STRATEGIES FOR
SUCCESS

STRATEGIES FOR SUCCESS

A Practical Guide to Learning English

H. Douglas Brown
San Francisco State University

Longman

Strategies for Success: A Practical Guide to Learning English

Pearson Education, 10 Bank Street, White Plains, NY 10606

Vice president, director of publishing: Allen Ascher
Editorial director: Louisa Hellegers
Acquisitions editor: Eleanor Kirby Barnes
Senior development manager: Penny Laporte
Development editor: Paula H. Van Ells
Vice president, director of design and production: Rhea Banker
Associate director of electronic production: Aliza Greenblatt
Executive managing editor: Linda Moser
Production manager: Ray Keating
Production editor: Janine DeFilippo
Director of manufacturing: Patrice Fraccio
Senior manufacturing buyer: Edie Pullman
Cover and text design: Ann France
Cover and text illustrations: Dusan Petricic
Text composition: Monika Popowitz

Library of Congress Cataloging-in-Publication Data
Brown, H. Douglas
    Strategies for success : a practical guide to learning English / H. Douglas Brown.
        p. cm.
ISBN 0-13-041392-5 (alk. paper)
1. English language—Textbooks for foreign speakers. 2. English language—Problems,
exercises, etc. I. Title.

PE1128 .B72495 2001
428.2'4—dc21

                                                 00-067385

  2 3 4 5 6 7 8 9 10—RRD—05 04 03 02 01

CONTENTS

Strategies-based instruction (SBI) is a relatively recent addition to the pedagogical storehouse of classroom teaching options. It has long been recognized that the most successful learners of languages are those who understand their own abilities and capacities well and who autonomously engage in systematic efforts within and beyond the classroom to reach self-determined goals of acquisition. However, SBI is difficult for many teachers to implement. Questions like the following are essential, but they are often obscured in teacher-training textbooks and in ESL/EFL textbooks.

- How do I teach learners to become aware of their styles?
- How can I get learners to practice good strategies?
- What are some effective classroom techniques for strategy training?

Strategies for Success: A Practical Guide to Learning English provides a pragmatic, teacher-friendly answer to those questions. It is easy for students to understand and use, and practical for you to incorporate into your classes. The book is designed to supplement an existing intermediate-level text in English as a second language (ESL) or English as a foreign language (EFL). Its twelve brief, simply written chapters offer a systematic program of strategies that will span most courses of study. About thirty minutes of reading weekly give students information about successful language-learning styles and strategies. Individual, partner, and group activities at the end of each chapter enable students to put into practice the concepts of the reading.

Features of *Strategies for Success*

Special features of this book include the following:

- Systematic learner-based strategies for use by English-language learners everywhere in virtually any classroom course of study
- Practical activities in the form of self-check questionnaires and end-of-chapter exercises
- Exercises that direct users to practice all four skills (listening, speaking, reading, and writing) as they develop successful strategies
- Partner learning activities, in which pairs of students follow step-by-step procedures
- Journal-writing exercises, in which each learner chronicles the process of self-discovery and strategy use

Using this book in your curriculum will occupy very little classroom time. Reading, vocabulary work, partner work, and journal writing can all, if you wish, be accomplished outside your class hours. Whole-class synthesis of each chapter might take ten to twenty minutes of class time.

Because strategies-based instruction is a relatively new facet of language teaching, students may at first find the notion of autonomous strategic planning to be mysterious and difficult. Teacher guidance, especially at the beginning, is therefore an important ingredient in starting students along their journey to self-awareness and strategic fulfillment of their goals.

If students in your classes follow this book with some commitment, you should find your classroom enriched by a more enthusiastic and inquisitive group of students, students who are beginning to take charge of their own learning. They will pick up strategic techniques for listening, speaking, reading, and writing English. They will feel empowered to learn for their own purposes. And they will be extending their English language learning into their own time beyond classroom hours.

How This Book Is Organized

Each chapter of *Strategies for Success* focuses on a different key concept in style awareness and strategy training.

- Chapter 1 introduces the notion that not all learners are the same in their preferences, and therefore it's important for each learner to know himself or herself well.
- Chapters 2 and 3 develop this theme through learning styles that have been shown to be crucial in learners' self-understanding.
- Chapters 4, 5, and 6 center on affective styles.
- Chapters 7, 8, and 9 point the learner to mental, linguistic, and cultural aspects of learning.
- Chapters 10 and 11 deal with individual and group strategies, respectively.
- Chapter 12 provides tips for taking tests successfully.

Each chapter offers students a self-check questionnaire, through which they learn something about their own preferences, styles, or habits. Specific strategy training is accomplished in end-of-chapter exercises that offer the following four types of processing:

1. Vocabulary and reading exercises lead students through a comprehensive check of the chapter (thereby practicing reading strategies).
2. Partners discuss key concepts and develop specific strategies to be utilized immediately (speaking and listening in the low-risk context of just two people).
3. Partner work is shared with the whole class, so that students can benefit from the collective wisdom of a larger group of learners (speaking to the whole class, a slightly higher-risk situation, and listening).

4. Finally, on their own, students log their strategy-learning process in a personal journal (low-risk freewriting strategies).

Conscientiously pursuing *Strategies for Success* leads students to awareness of their own unique styles and proclivities and to strategies for many learning contexts and skill areas. One of the tangible benefits will be many different *lists* of strategies (written on Post-it® notes for easy placement on bulletin boards, walls, notebook covers) readily accessible for current and future language courses.

How to Use This Book in Your Class

Here are some generic suggestions for using *Strategies for Success* in your current English language course. In the first chapter or two of the book, you will need to spend a little time walking students through the process.

Teachers of pilot editions of this material successfully used the following procedures early in the course:

Before Chapter 1

- Tell students to read (or skim) *To the Student* (page xiii).
- Perform an oral whole-class comprehension check with the following questions:

    1. What do successful students do to learn English really well?
    2. What is a "strategy"?
    3. How is this book different from your regular textbook?
    4. What is a learning partner?
    5. What is a journal, and what will you write in it?
    6. What are Post-it notes, and how will you use them?

Chapters 1 and 2

- Encourage students by telling them how important it is to understand their own preferences and to develop strategies that are in harmony with their preferences.
- Ask students to predict the focus of a chapter by looking at the title.
- Make sure students understand how to fill out the questionnaires. Stress the fact that there are no "right" or "wrong" answers and that their honest opinion about themselves will benefit them the most.
- Assign the chapter as homework reading (if time permits, reading could be done in class). Encourage reading the first time through without looking up unknown words in a dictionary.
- Make sure students understand the directions in each of the four exercises.
- Facilitate the formation of pairs for partner work (whether partner-work exercises are done in class or after class).

- Monitor partner work.
- Make sure students understand how to use Post-its in making lists of strategies, and suggest places where they might put them in order to be regularly reminded of them.
- Set aside class time for the exercise *Discussing with the Whole Class.*
- Help students to get started writing a journal (buying a notebook, telling them what sorts of things they should write).
- Consider asking students to hand in their journals every few weeks so that you can follow their progress and make comments and suggestions. Grading journals is not recommended since it could inhibit students' writing.

Chapters 3–12

Your role as a teacher can be less central as students understand the routine of reading, filling out questionnaires, and doing the exercises. The amount of attention you pay will vary, depending on the students and the curriculum. When class time is used for the exercises, of course, your leadership is essential. Of great importance is your continued conviction that what students are doing is productive! Show your own enthusiasm for the spirit of *Strategies for Success* with steady encouragement and praise throughout the term.

Connecting *Strategies for Success* to Your Regular Course

You can reinforce students' increasing style awareness and their enlarging storehouse of strategies in a number of ways as you pursue your course objectives.

1. Incorporate words, concepts, and principles from *Strategies for Success* into impromptu examples and illustrations of the grammar, pronunciation, vocabulary, and communication exercises of your regular course. Some examples are:

   - Used to: "I used to be a low-risk taker."
   - Pronunciation practice: /l/ vs. /r/: "left brain and right brain"
   - Vocabulary: "internal" and "external"
   - Discourse: complimenting others—"Your English is really good! You must have high self-confidence."

2. Use the results of the questionnaires to guide your teaching approach. For example, if you find that most of your students are reflective learners, you might (a) offer enough classroom work to help reflective learners feel comfortable expressing themselves aloud and (b) also help reflectives develop a faster response through fluency exercises.

3. Recognize the diversity of styles in your class by offering diverse forms of activities both to stay in the "comfort zone" of students and to challenge them to reach beyond their current preferences.

4. The end-of-chapter exercise *Understanding Reading and Vocabulary* provides progressive practice in guessing words in context, reading for the gist, and other reading strategies. If your course has a reading focus, these exercises are a good reinforcement for reading strategies. If not, call attention to the importance of reading strategically when students are reading other material.

5. In some cases, the end-of-chapter exercise *Discussing with the Whole Class* may be modified to fit into some other aspect of your regular curriculum.

6. Journal writing might be an appropriate context in which students practice writing that's related to your course goals. The journal could then serve a dual purpose.

Acknowledgments

Strategies for Success: A Practical Guide to Learning English is the result of over a decade of experiment and trial. The first seeds were planted with the publication of my *Practical Guide to Language Learning* (McGraw-Hill, 1989), which has been successfully used by American college students studying various foreign languages (French, Spanish, Italian, and so on). However, the current book is a markedly different volume, not only in its targeting of English as a second/foreign language, but also from having benefited from a decade of further research on strategies-based instruction and from multiple revisions of its pilot versions.

Some earlier versions, including translations, of the present book were test-taught and reviewed in Brazil, Hong Kong, Thailand, and Japan. I am grateful to the many teachers in those four countries for their useful feedback. Special thanks go to faculty members and students at the Chinese University of Hong Kong and to teachers connected with the teacher education seminar at Uniao Cultural Brasil-Estados Unidos in 1997. Editions translated into Japanese by Kensaku Yoshida and into Thai by Kanittha Navarat provided a further source of information on market and suitability.

The most closely monitored pilot program using a previous version of *Strategies for Success* was conducted at the American Language Institute at San Francisco State University. For this I am thankful for the work of my graduate thesis student Hitomi Takahashi, who taught and tracked students through a semester-long process. I am further grateful to Kathy Sherak and Peg Sarosy, my colleagues at the American Language Institute, for their comments and encouragement. Also, I appreciate the contribution of Amy Shipley for her ideas for some of the illustrations in this book. Finally, many thanks to Eleanor Barnes, my editor at Pearson Education, for believing in this project, for helping me set the tone for the book, for devoting so much effort to myriad bits and pieces of detailed feedback, and for sharing her own experience in teaching and publishing.

H. Douglas Brown

Do you want to improve your English? Do you want to speak English fluently? Do you want to use English someday in your work or in your school? Do you want to pass an English examination? Your answers to these questions probably are yes. How can you do all this? According to scientific studies, successful students spend a lot of time doing the following things:

- Setting *goals* on their own
- *Practicing* with other people outside of class
- *Analyzing* their own mistakes in conversations
- Using many different *strategies* for learning

Strategies are techniques that you can use to make yourself a more successful learner. Strategies include ideas for practicing conversations, ways to learn vocabulary, suggestions for reading English, techniques for listening to English, and guidelines for writing English.

It's difficult to learn a language really well. But with the help of the strategies that this book will teach you, you too can become successful! As you do the exercises in this book, you will gradually become a better English learner. You will be successful if you do the following:

- Think positively.
- Take responsibility for your learning.
- Make an effort to learn.
- Don't depend on the teacher for everything.

How to Use This Book

This book can be used with your regular English textbook. Each short chapter has some ideas for you to think about. The exercises at the end of each chapter help you to *practice* those ideas. You will learn English better in your classroom and also outside your classroom.

Here's how to use the book:

- Each week, read one chapter.
- Guess at or look up words you don't understand.
- Talk with another student about meanings you don't understand.
- Do the exercises at the end of each chapter.

Some of the exercises are things to do in class that your teacher can help you with. The others should be done outside classroom time; you will need to plan on spending a little extra time every week outside class working on your English.

Working with a Partner

Most students learn better by working with a classmate. This book gives you exercises that you can do with a *learning partner*, a classmate to talk with and work with. Your teacher can help you to choose a *learning partner*.

You and your *learning partner* should do the following things:

- Meet together once a week for about an hour.
- Make sure you both understand everything in the chapter.
- Check the meaning of vocabulary you do not know.
- Do the exercises for *learning partners*.

Keeping a Journal

One exercise at the end of each chapter gives you topics to write about in a *journal*. A journal is a very informal diary about your own feelings and thoughts as you study English. It's easy to write a journal and it will help you to be a better student.

Here's how to write your journal:

- Buy a notebook that is strong and easy to carry with you.
- Write your name and the title, *My Strategies for Success*, on the cover of the notebook.
- Each time you write in it, record the date.
- Write answers to the questions in the journal exercises at the end of each chapter.
- Write other lists and ideas, if you want to, for the other exercises.
- Write as much or as little as you want to—a sentence or two or several pages. It's your choice.
- Don't worry about grammar and spelling.
- Look back every few weeks at what you have written.

Write something in your journal, for about ten or fifteen minutes, at least once a week—more often if you can. Writing helps you to express your thoughts and feelings about yourself as an English learner. By thinking about your learning, you'll be able to see which strategies work best for you and which don't work. At the end of the course, you will be able to see your progress.

Using Post-its and Reminders

Some of the exercises in this book recommend that you make lists of strategies. One useful way to make these lists is to write them on Post-its, to put in places where you can see them every day. Stick them in your notebook, or textbook, on your computer, desk, mirror, and so on. These notes will remind you to practice strategies while you learn English.

Conclusion

You can be more successful by spending a little extra time outside class practicing and using English. If you believe in yourself and follow the suggestions in this book, you will discover that the extra effort is rewarding!

Good luck to you!

H. Douglas Brown

1 | What Kind of Learner Are You?

There are many different kinds of learners. Some are fast and some are slow. Some learners like numbers and some like words. Some students are good at memorizing word for word; others are good at remembering general ideas. When studying English, some students find it easy to talk and other students prefer to listen. Some people are embarrassed easily, and some don't care if people laugh at them. All these differences are not "bad" or "good." They are just differences. However, it's important for you to understand *yourself* in order to be successful.

What kind of learner are you? What do you think you like and don't like about learning English? What do you prefer?

To start finding out about your own preferences, do Questionnaire 1. If you don't know the meaning of a word or phrase, try to guess it or ask your teacher or look it up in a dictionary.

QUESTIONNAIRE 1 Learner Preferences

Circle the letter for each sentence that best describes you. Circle only one letter for each item. Use the following scale:

A   *The sentence on the left describes you well.*

B   *The sentence on the left somewhat describes you.*

C   *The sentence on the right somewhat describes you.*

D   *The sentence on the right describes you well.*

- -

Example

| I love watching baseball games. | **A** (**B**) **C** **D** | I hate watching baseball games. |

Letter B has been circled. This means that this person is somewhat interested in watching baseball.

- -

1. I don't mind if people laugh when I speak English.	**A B C D**	I get embarrassed if people laugh when I speak English.
2. I study English outside class, on my own.	**A B C D**	I study English in class only, when the teacher tells me to.
3. I like to get the general idea when I read or listen to English.	**A B C D**	I must understand every word when I read or listen to English.
4. When I make a mistake, I don't get upset because I can learn from my mistakes.	**A B C D**	When I make a mistake, I get upset and feel that I have failed.
5. I enjoy working in groups.	**A B C D**	I prefer to work alone.

Look at the questionnaire. For each item, if you circled *A* or *B*, underline the sentence on the left; and if you circled *C* or *D*, underline the sentence on the right.

Questionnaire 1 tells you what your *preferences* are in learning English. For example, for the first item, if you underlined the statement on the left, "I don't mind if people laugh when I speak English," you are indicating that you are comfortable taking risks and trying out your English; if someone laughs at you, you will continue to speak without worrying too much about yourself. If you circled the sentence on the right, "I get embarrassed if people laugh when I speak English," you are probably quite sensitive to other people's reactions to you. You are probably a little shy, and if people laugh at you, you think that they don't think you're very smart.

Generally, the five statements on the left are preferences you will want to develop. Items you circled on the right are preferences you should probably try to change. For most people, success comes faster with the preferences on the left.

When you do the exercises at the end of this chapter, you will probably discover that you are different in some ways from other students in your class. You will find out that people's preferences for learning languages vary. In the exercises, you will have a chance to talk and then write about the results of Questionnaire 1. In the rest of this book, principles of successful language learning will be discussed, and you will develop strategies for more self-discovery and for action.

EXERCISES

Understanding Reading and Vocabulary

To help you to understand the chapter better, do the following on your own.

1. Read the chapter again and circle any words you don't understand.
2. Guess the meaning of each word by looking at the rest of the sentence or paragraph.
3. In your notebook, make a list of words you still do not know.
4. Look them up in a dictionary and write the definitions in your notebook.
5. Read the sentences with the words you don't know again. You should now understand these sentences better.

Speaking and Listening with a Partner

A. Ask each other the following questions. Try to get as much information as possible about your partner.

1. Where are you from? Do you like your hometown?
2. Who are your family members?
3. What do your parents do?
4. What are your interests and hobbies?
5. How much English have you studied?
6. Why are you in this English class?

B. Look again at Questionnaire 1 on page 2. Discuss each of the five items in the questionnaire.

1. Tell your partner why you underlined the sentence you did.
2. Give examples of your preference from your own learning of English.

3. Are you successful with each of your preferences, compared to the preference on the other side?
4. Take turns giving advice to your partner about how to become more successful in learning English.
5. Together, think of three or four rules for successful language learning that use the preferences you have just discussed, for example: "I study English outside class, on my own." Write these rules on a Post-it®. Put the Post-it where you will see it often: on a notebook cover, a textbook cover, a desk, a mirror, or a bulletin board.

Discussing with the Whole Class

Tell the class your rules. If you like any rules other students made, write them down in your notebook, and try to follow them.

Writing Your Journal

Choose *two* items from Questionnaire 1, and write answers to these questions for each item.

1. Which sentence did you underline? Why?
2. Give an example that illustrates your preference.

2 Discovering Your Learning Styles

Read about two different students in the same English class.

Student 1

Maria is eighteen years old and wants to go to a university in the United States. She has been an excellent student all her life, getting lots of A's on her report cards. In her English class, she is very shy. She seldom speaks in class unless the teacher calls on her. Whenever she speaks English, she likes to plan what she is going to say, so she takes a long time to say things. Her English has good grammar, but her pronunciation is not very clear. She prefers to write things down in English before saying them. She has high scores on her written quizzes and tests, but her scores on pronunciation quizzes are only average. She studies very hard, by herself, outside class. She almost never goes to parties.

Student 2

Manuel is also eighteen years old and also wants to go to a university in the United States. His grades in school have been average. In his English class he talks a lot. He always raises his hand to speak. He never really plans what he is going to say. His grammar is average, but his pronunciation is excellent and he talks very naturally. He doesn't write things down very often. His written test scores are average, but on pronunciation quizzes he usually gets an A+. Outside class, Manuel rarely studies, but he has a lot of American friends and talks with them a lot. He loves to go to parties.

Which student is more successful, Maria or Manuel? It is difficult to answer this question because they are both good in different skills in English. They both have different *learning styles*. Learning styles are ways of remembering thoughts and ideas and of practicing skills. Almost always, your own learning style will be a little different from someone else's. Here are some different learning styles:

Some people	**Other people**
use their eyes	use their ears
write things down	listen carefully
work fast	work slowly
say things without thinking	say things only after thinking a lot
learn by doing	learn by analyzing and thinking
enjoy exact rules	enjoy general guidelines
practice with other people	practice alone

You have your own set of learning styles. You have developed your styles over many years. However, you can change a learning style if you decide that it is important to change it. For example, if you have always learned well by studying alone and memorizing words and grammar, you might discover that you can learn to *speak* English better by talking with others and by not worrying about exact grammar. However, if you love to talk a lot but your grammar is bad, you might need to pay more attention to correct grammar.

Many years of research have shown that one group of learning styles is not best for foreign language learning.

STRATEGIES FOR SUCCESS

Successful language learners usually

- understand their own learning styles and preferences.
- know which styles *help* them and use those styles.
- know which styles might *hurt* them and change or avoid those styles.

Before you read further, do Questionnaire 2.

QUESTIONNAIRE 2   Slow or Fast?

Circle the number that best describes how quickly you usually do things. Circle only one number for each item. Use the following scale:

1 *Very fast*
2 *Fast*
3 *In between*
4 *Slow*
5 *Very slow*

Example

How fast or slow I usually am when I . . .

Do my homework   1 ② 3 4 5

Number 2 has been circled. This means that this person does homework quite fast and takes less time than most classmates.

How fast or slow I usually am when I . . .

1. Read books, magazines, and newspapers in English   1 2 3 4 5

2. Read textbooks, articles, and reports in English, in my
   academic field   1 2 3 4 5

3. Write an essay or composition in English   1 2 3 4 5

4. Take multiple-choice tests in English   1 2 3 4 5

5. Answer tests in English that ask for written sentences or
   paragraphs   1 2 3 4 5

6. Answer a direct question to me from the teacher, in my
   English class   1 2 3 4 5

7. Raise my hand when the teacher asks a question in my
   English class   1 2 3 4 5

8. Volunteer to say something in class, when the teacher has
   not asked me   1 2 3 4 5

9. Speak up in a small group in English, in class   1 2 3 4 5

10. Answer a question in English from someone outside my
    classroom   1 2 3 4 5

Add up the numbers you circled. You should get a total score between 10 and 50.

Score: _____

Questionnaire 2 tells you if you are usually slow or fast when you are working on your English. Are you a slow or a fast reader? Are you usually the first or the last one to put your hand up and speak up in a classroom? Do you like to make sure you're right before saying or writing something, or do you usually make a lot of little guesses, even though you might be wrong? One important learning style is *speed*, that is, how slow or fast someone is. If you prefer doing things more slowly, your style is *reflective*. If you like to do things fast, your style is *impulsive*.

Look again at your total score on Questionnaire 2. This is what your score means:

Score

30 or more   You are a *reflective* learner. You like to think about things before making a decision; you want to make sure you are right before speaking. The higher your score, the more reflective you are.

29 or less   You are *impulsive*. You make quick decisions and are willing to gamble that you are right. The lower your score, the more impulsive you are.

Reflective people usually like to think quite a lot before making a decision. They need to be certain of the right answer before trying it out. They slowly move ahead in logical steps. They're usually slower readers, who want to make sure that they understand what they're reading before continuing. Consequently, they usually make fewer comprehension errors in reading.

On the other hand, impulsive learners are faster thinkers. They usually enjoy making guesses. They are also willing to be wrong sometimes. They are usually fast readers since they often ignore words or phrases that they don't immediately understand and just continue reading. While they make more errors in reading, they are often good at guessing the meanings of words and sentences.

Should you try to be faster? Or should you slow down a little? It depends. Both styles have advantages and disadvantages.

	Reflective Style	**Impulsive Style**
Advantages	More accurate speaking More accurate reading Think carefully before acting	More willing to speak in class Faster reading Better in timed tests
Disadvantages	Wait too long to speak Read more slowly Slower in timed tests	Less accurate in speaking Less accurate in reading Act without thinking enough

There are advantages and disadvantages to whichever style you have. Many English learners are too reflective when they speak. They wait too long while they try to think of the right word or grammar pattern before speaking. These learners should try to be more impulsive so that they can speed up. Be careful, though, because being too impulsive can hurt you. If you speak English without thinking about what you want to say, people might not understand you.

Of course, your goal is balance: to be not too fast, not too slow. If your score on Questionnaire 2 was 46 to 50 or 10 to 14, you should aim for more balance in your decision-making speed. You need to have the courage to make some guesses, but you should also take some time for reflection. Remember, however, that neither style is necessarily good or bad.

EXERCISES

Understanding Reading and Vocabulary

A. Answer these questions in your notebook:
1. What is a learning style?
2. How are Maria's and Manuel's learning styles different from each other?
3. On page 6 is a list of examples of different learning styles. Which styles describe you better?
4. Which things do you think you should try to change? Explain your reasons.
5. What does it mean to be *balanced* between reflective and impulsive learning styles?

B. Circle any words in this chapter that you don't understand. With a partner, guess the meanings of the words from their context (sentences before and after). Try not to use a dictionary.

Speaking and Listening with a Partner

Look at your score on Questionnaire 2 on page 7, and ask your partner these questions.
1. Is your style reflective or impulsive?
2. Do you think your score describes your learning style well?
3. What are some things you do while learning English that are examples of your style (reflective or impulsive)?
4. What do you think you should change in your style in order to be more successful? Make a short list of changes. (For ideas, look at the chart on page 8, which lists advantages and disadvantages). Why do you think you should make those changes?

Discussing with the Whole Class

Share your list from the last exercise with the rest of the class. Then make a class list of five to ten things that everyone recommends to help students to be successful. Put this list on the board or on a large piece of cardboard or posterboard to keep in front of your classroom.

Writing Your Journal

A. Look at item 4 in *Speaking and Listening with a Partner* on page 9. Write a list of specific things that you will do to balance reflective and impulsive learning.

Examples

I will volunteer to speak in class once each day this week.

I will think carefully about what I'm going to say and how I'm going to say it before I start speaking.

Write this list on a Post-it note. Then put it on a desk, a wall, a bulletin board, a mirror, or a book where you won't forget it. Look at the list regularly. Practice the things on the list.

B. Think about all the classes you have taken in English. Write a paragraph that describes your style as a language learner. Your paragraph may look like the ones that described Maria and Manuel. Try to describe your learning styles as completely as possible.

3 Left Brain and Right Brain

Right brain: Wide-angle lens

Left brain: Zoom lens

When you were five years old, you probably used your native language all the time. But did you think about grammar rules? Did you worry about correct pronunciation or using verbs and articles correctly? Of course not. And if you learned a foreign language when you were young, you didn't think about rules and grammar in that language either. You learned languages naturally, without thinking about the language.

But now you're an adult, and you probably analyze English a lot. Perhaps you memorize lists of words, learn grammar rules, look up words in a dictionary, and translate from one language to the other. You probably know more about the rules of English than about how to speak it or read it fluently. You may be thinking too much about the details of English grammar and pronunciation; you may need to be a little childlike when you use English.

What's Your Learning Focus?

Think of language learning as using a camera with interchangeable lenses. You can use a zoom lens to focus on the details of English—what every word means, how every rule is applied, and what all the exceptions are. You can use a wide-angle lens to see the general meaning of something—the big picture of what someone is trying to say or write.

Adults usually use the zoom lens a little too much when they learn languages. Children usually use a wide-angle lens as they learn a language naturally. As an adult, you must make a conscious effort to use a wide-angle lens most of the time, only occasionally zooming in on a word or grammar point.

You can also think of learning English as similar to learning to play a sport. If you think about it too much, it doesn't work. I used to overanalyze my tennis game. I would tell myself to watch the ball or to swing the racket correctly or to change my grip for a backhand shot. But I analyzed so much that I couldn't relax and just play the game! I was too aware of myself. I finally discovered that I was more successful if I focused on the big picture: the game, not myself.

Should you stop studying grammar, pronunciation, and vocabulary? No! Focusing on the small pieces of English is important and useful. It helps you to see what you can't see with your wide-angle lens. As you continue to learn English, it's very useful to be able to quickly zoom in on a difficult word or grammar point, and then to zoom out to the wider angle again.

Adults have an advantage over children here. Children have only the wide-angle lens; they learn languages *subconsciously*. Adults can do both: we can learn both subconsciously and *consciously*. Research shows that being able to learn both ways is important for success. You need to be childlike enough to relax with the language and not be too worried about all the details. But at the right times, you also need to examine your language with your zoom lens, then use the detail to improve your language.

Here's an example of what it's like to use a wide-angle lens when you look at things. Look at the row of strange shapes below. Can you read the message? What does it say? Don't read further until you have tried this puzzle for a few minutes.

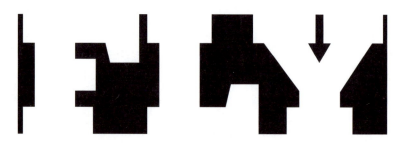

Did you get it? You have to look at the white spaces between the black shapes. The three white spaces are the three letters, F, L, and Y, spelling the word FLY. You may have looked at the black shapes because you are used to seeing black print on white paper. Don't be tricked!

This puzzle is an example of how you can focus on the wrong thing in a language if you don't have a wide-angle view of language. If you look too closely at the puzzle, you focus on the details. If you back away and look at the whole picture, you get it. Language works the same way.

Before you read further, do Questionnaire 3.

QUESTIONNAIRE 3 Left-Brain and Right-Brain Processing

Circle the number that best describes you. Circle only one number for each item. Use the following scale:

1   *The sentence on the left describes you well.*

2   *The sentence on the left somewhat describes you.*

3   *The sentence on the right somewhat describes you.*

4   *The sentence on the right describes you well.*

Example

I prefer speaking to large groups.   **1 2 ③ 4**   I prefer speaking to small groups.

Number 3 has been circled. This means that this person somewhat prefers speaking in small group situations.

----

1. I try to make decisions based on facts.   **1 2 3 4**   I make decisions based on my feelings.

2. I like rules and exact information.   **1 2 3 4**   I like general guidelines and uncertain information.

3. I like to solve a problem by first looking at all its parts.   **1 2 3 4**   I like to solve a problem by looking at the whole problem.

4. I read slowly and try to carefully analyze what I am reading.   **1 2 3 4**   I read fast and try to get the general meaning of what I am reading.

5. I like teachers to tell me exactly what to do.   **1 2 3 4**   I like teachers to give me a lot of freedom to choose what I can do.

6. I like mathematics and science.   **1 2 3 4**   I like literature and art.

7. When I listen, I pay attention to people's exact words.   **1 2 3 4**   When I listen, I pay attention to the overall message.

8. I like multiple-choice tests.   **1 2 3 4**   I like open-ended essay tests.

Add up the numbers you circled. You should get a total score between 8 and 32.

Score: ____

Questionnaire 3 tells you if you use *left-brain* processing or *right-brain* processing more. The brain is divided into two parts. The left brain is like the zoom lens. It is logical, analytical, and mathematical. The right brain is like the wide-angle lens. It is better at remembering social, emotional, and artistic experiences. Left-brain and right-brain processing involve a whole set of style differences.

Very young children tend to use their right brain more. Then, as they grow older, the left brain develops. As an adult, people use one side or the other side most. Do you remember reading in the last chapter about reflective and impulsive styles? Left-brain and right-brain preferences work the same way as styles: you probably use one side of your brain more than the other.

Your brain processing preference was measured in Questionnaire 3. This is what your score means:

Score

28-32	High right-brain preference
23-27	Moderate right-brain preference
18-22	No particular preference for either side
13-17	Moderate left-brain preference
8-12	High left-brain preference

Interpret your score from the questionnaire using the following chart.

Left Brain	**Right Brain**
Zoom lens	Wide-angle lens
Rules and definitions	General guidelines
Logical, systematic, planned	Intuitive, flexible, spontaneous
Language, mathematics	Music, art
Focuses on details	Gets the general idea

Balancing Your Brain

So what does all this mean to *you* and your English study? According to some research studies, people who learn foreign languages outside the classroom use the right brain more in the beginning than when they are at advanced levels. People may naturally use wide-angle lenses when they are beginning a language and use zoom lenses more when they reach a higher ability. But many English language classes do just the opposite! They teach the details of English grammar at the beginning. Much later in the process, students are expected to get a "feel" for the language. This means that many students are being taught to learn English backwards. It is better to get general meanings with the right brain early in the course and to focus on grammar and vocabulary and so on later.

In your English classes, you may have been using your left brain by focusing on the details instead of being more relaxed and childlike. You might become a better learner by using more of your right brain.

On the other hand, it's important to remember that the left and right sides of your brain work together as a team. Most of the time, when we are learning something, we use both the left and right brain. We do some analyzing, find rules, and focus on details, *and* we use our intuition and get general meanings. Often we find the best answers to problems by using both sides of the brain.

Remember, it's important for you to know which side of the brain you usually use more, but it's also important for you to use *both* sides of your brain, depending on the situation. Your left and right brain are members of a *team*. Use both sides and your brain will stay balanced!

EXERCISES

Understanding Reading and Vocabulary

Here are some words from this chapter that help you to understand left-brain and right-brain learning styles.

conscious	intuitive
subconscious	spontaneous
logical	systematic

With a partner, do the following for each word:

1. Find and circle the word in the chapter. Look at the word's context.
2. Define the word by looking at the context. If you still cannot define it, then look it up in a dictionary.
3. Take turns using the word in sentences that show the word's meanings.
4. After you have done this exercise with your partner, then, on your own, write down in your notebook the six words and the sentences you made with your partner.

Speaking and Listening with a Partner

Look at your score for Questionnaire 3 on page 13, and then discuss the following:

1. According to the questionnaire, which do you use more, your left brain or right brain? Do you agree?
2. What are some things you do while learning English that are examples of left-brain and right-brain styles?
3. Make a list of specific things you could do to improve use of the left side of your brain and things you could do to improve use of the right side your brain.

Example

Left-brain things I could do	_Right-brain things I could do_
_Pay more attention to my pronunciation of _____._	_Read faster and skip words that I don't know._

4. Copy your lists onto Post-its and stick them near the other Post-it lists you have been making.

Discussing with the Whole Class

Share your lists from _Speaking and Listening with a Partner_ with the rest of the class. As other classmates are sharing their lists, write down any of their ideas that you would like to add to your list. Write the lists on the board. When everyone has shared their lists, if time permits, tell the class what ideas, if any, you added to your list.

Writing Your Journal

Write about things you have done in your English classes that you think were either helpful or not helpful.

Example

When I was in high school, I remember my teacher used

to make us learn the grammar rules that we were studying.

We had to write the rules down in our tests. For example, we

learned that the present perfect tense expresses an action

that began in the past and is continuing in the present.

The funny thing is, we focused on the rules but could never

use them when we were speaking English.

4 Motivating Yourself and Setting Goals

What does it mean to be *motivated* to learn something? Motivation is one of the most important factors in your success in English. Motivation means having a real purpose in learning English, or really wanting to learn English for a reason. Some people are very strongly motivated to learn a language. Others are not, and others are in between. Sometimes someone else, such as a parent or teacher, is pushing a person to learn English.

What is your motivation for learning English? Are you learning English because you are being pushed by parents, teachers, or school requirements? Or are you learning because you want to learn for your own purposes and reasons? Both of these motives are important to understand as you continue to learn English.

Before you read further, do Questionnaire 4.

QUESTIONNAIRE 4   Two Kinds of Motivation

Circle the number that best describes how you feel about learning English. Circle only one number for each item. Use the following scale. Be honest!

4   *I strongly agree. This statement describes me very well.*

3   *I somewhat agree. This statement probably describes me.*

2   *I somewhat disagree. This statement probably does not describe me.*

1   *I strongly disagree. This statement definitely does not describe me.*

Example

I want to learn English well so that I can marry a Canadian and live in Canada.   **4 ③ 2 1**

Number 3 has been circled. This means that this statement somewhat describes this person.

Part I

1. I want to learn English well so that I can talk with native speakers of English.   **4 3 2 1**

2. I have set my own goals for learning English and want to be successful in reaching those goals.   **4 3 2 1**

3. English will help me to get a good job someday.   **4 3 2 1**

4. English will help me to be successful in my studies.   **4 3 2 1**

5. I hope to meet (or have already met) a special friend who speaks English.   **4 3 2 1**

Part II

6. I am studying English because it is a required course in my school or university.   **4 3 2 1**

7. I need to pass an English proficiency test (like the TOEFL or an entrance exam).   **4 3 2 1**

8. My parents want me to learn English, so I'm here to please them.   **4 3 2 1**

9. I am studying English because I want to please my teacher and get good grades.   **4 3 2 1**

10. I am studying English because most of my friends are good in English.   **4 3 2 1**

Add up the numbers you circled in each part. You should get a total score between 5 and 20 for each part.

Scores: Part I _____   Part II _____

On Questionnaire 4 you got two scores. Each score tells you where your motivation comes from. Your score on Part I tells you how strongly your motivation comes from inside yourself. If your score was between 13 and 20, your motivation to learn English comes strongly from *inside* yourself: you are learning English for your own reasons and purposes. If your score on Part I was between 5 and 12, your own reasons and purposes for learning English are not very strong.

Your score on Part II tells you how strongly other influences are pushing you to learn English. If your score was between 16 and 25, you are very strongly motivated by other influences. If your score was between 5 and 15, you are not strongly motivated by what other people want you to do.

Now look again at your scores on Questionnaire 4. This is what your scores mean:

Score	Part I	Part II
13-20	High self-motivation	High motivation from others
5-12	Low self-motivation	Low motivation from others

Internal and External Motivation

Now you're going to learn two important terms that will help you to understand yourself and to become more successful in the future: *internal* motivation and *external* motivation.

Self-motivation is internal, and motivation from others is external. Internal motivation means that you are doing something because you want to do it or because you have made your own choice to do it; you don't need a reward from someone else to do well. Your success is your reward; just knowing that you have learned something pleases you. Research has found that when people are motivated by their own wants and needs they are almost always successful.

External motivation is when other influences, such as teachers or school requirements, push you to do something. In this case, you often need to receive rewards, such as good grades, high scores, and praise. Without rewards, you may not be motivated enough to study English very hard. People who are motivated by outside influences are usually not so successful, because their reason for learning does not come from inside them.

Examples of internal motivation

- You decide to clean up your room because you want it to be neat.
- You do your homework assignment because you are interested in the topic.
- You finish your company's project because you can learn from it.
- You don't smoke cigarettes because they are unhealthy for you.
- You buy a new car because you really need one and can pay for it.
- You take English so that you can understand people in many countries.

Examples of external motivation

- You clean your room because your parents tell you to do it.
- You do your homework assignment because your teacher tells you to do it.
- You finish a project on time to please your boss.
- You smoke cigarettes because many people around you smoke.
- You buy a new car because a TV ad tells you you must have a new car.
- You take English to pass an entrance exam.

If you develop internal motivation to learn something, you will keep on learning for a long time, and you will learn more. If you have only external motivation to learn, you will depend on other people to reward you or you won't continue to learn.

Many countries require students to study English in junior high and senior high school. You may have already taken many years of English as a student. If those years of English classes were forced on you, your motivation was probably external and therefore quite weak. You succeeded because you wanted to get a good grade or pass an exam, not because you yourself wanted to improve your English. But if you had your own reasons and rewards for learning English and you believed the language would be important to you, then your motivation was more internal and probably stronger.

What did the questionnaire scores show about your internal and external motivation? The exercises at the end of this chapter will help you to become more self-motivated. If you can develop internal reasons (I want to do it for myself, not just for my teacher or my school) for learning English, you will almost always have greater and more satisfying success.

Many students learning English today are in an English course because of a requirement. But the most successful students will change their external reasons for learning English into internal reasons. If your only reasons for learning English are external, you can change them. Here are some possible ways.

STRATEGIES FOR SUCCESS

1. Think about your motives right now.

- The course is required.
- You care a lot about your grades.
- You have to pass an exam at the end.
- You have to pass the TOEFL.

2. Make a list of internal reasons to learn English.

- You will succeed better in school later on.
- You will do better in your job.
- You will have more fun talking with English speakers.
- You will be able to use the Internet better.

3. **Set some specific goals for yourself to pursue in the next few weeks.**

   • I will use the Internet to write English e-mail messages to people.

4. **Look at your goals frequently and track your progress.**

5. **As you complete goals, set new ones.**

English Around the World Today

English has become the international language for communication around the world. This might be an excellent internal reason for you to learn English. Just about everywhere you go in the world today, you can find people who speak English. People in airports and taxis and hotels are able to speak to you in English.

Think about these points:

• Over 1 billion people use English in the world today.
• Companies around the world require English for many job positions.
• Airlines and travel agencies like to employ people who have English skills.
• Many countries have English TV and radio stations.
• Most Web sites are in English.
• Universities around the world use textbooks and reports written in English.

Do these points give you reasons to set your own goals? Can you see how they might help you to be more internally motivated to work hard on learning English? The following exercises will give you some specific ways to develop a stronger internal motive for learning English.

EXERCISES

Understanding Reading and Vocabulary

On your own, go through this chapter and make a list of any words you do not know. Then, with a partner, do the following:

1. Pick ten words from your list and your partner's list.
2. Help each other to define the words.
3. In your notebook, each of you write a new sentence using each word.

Speaking and Listening with a Partner

Compare your scores from Questionnaire 4 on page 18. In the following chart, circle "High" or "Low" for each type of motivation.

Internal motivation	**External motivation**
13–20 High	13–20 High
5–12 Low	5–12 Low

Now answer these questions.

1. What are your internal and external reasons for taking this English class?
2. What are two or three things you can do to make yourself more internally motivated?

Examples

I will study for myself, not to please my teacher.

I will study for my future, not just to pass the next test.

I will set goals for myself every week.

3. Write your own list of goals on a Post-it. Put the Post-it where you will see it often to remind you to work on your goals.

Discussing with the Whole Class

Look at the list of examples of the use of English around the world today on page 21. Divide up into groups of four.

1. Discuss what parts of your (future) job may require speaking, listening, reading, or writing in English.

Examples

If you plan to start a business of your own, how will English help you?

If you want to be a computer scientist, what tasks will you need to do in English?

2. Report your findings to the rest of your class.

Writing Your Journal

Now make a list in your journal of some specific goals to follow in the next few weeks and specific things you can do to reach these goals.

Examples

Goal: *I will make a score of _____ on the test at the end of the semester.*

Actions: *1. I will read _____ pages (beyond my classwork and homework) in English every week (from a newspaper, magazine, or book).*

2. I will listen to (on the radio) or watch (on TV) _____ hours of English a week.

Copy these goals on a Post-it or two. Then put them where you will see them every day. Set aside some time every day to work on your goals. First look at your daily schedule and decide how much time you can spend (ten minutes, fifteen minutes, one hour). Try to work on your goals at the same time every day so that you establish a routine. This will make it easier for you to continue to do the things that will help you reach your goals.

5 Developing Self-Confidence and Lowering Anxiety

By now, you know enough English to read this book, write a few paragraphs, and speak in some social situations. But you still may not be confident of your mastery of the English language. Learning a new language involves many things:

- Learning a whole new system of sounds
- Remembering thousands of new words
- Learning many, many rules of grammar—and their exceptions
- Talking with people in different situations (friends, teachers, etc.)
- Understanding a new culture

Do you think you will learn all these things some day? If so, great! Don't lose your self-confidence. Sometimes you might think, "I'm not sure I can learn all these things. Will I ever be able to speak, listen to, read, and write English really well?" The answer to these questions is yes. Think about these points:

- Little children learn other languages without even studying them.
- Research has shown that you don't have to be an A+ student in school to learn a foreign language well. Anyone can learn another language.
- In many parts of the world people are bilingual, so learning another language is a very natural thing.
- Teenagers and adults who go to live in other countries almost always learn the country's language if they think positively and practice it a lot.

How confident are you about your English? Do you believe in yourself? Before you read further, do Questionnaire 5.

QUESTIONNAIRE 5   General Self-Confidence

Circle the number that best describes how you feel about yourself most of the time. Circle only one number for each item. Use the following scale:

4   *I strongly agree. This statement describes me very well.*

3   *I somewhat agree. This statement probably describes me.*

2   *I somewhat disagree. This statement probably does not describe me.*

1   *I strongly disagree. This statement definitely does not describe me.*

Example

I am afraid a lot of the time.   **4 3 2 (1)**

Number 1 has been circled. This means that this person strongly disagrees and thinks that this statement does not describe him or her very well.

----

1. I understand my own personality.   **4 3 2 1**

2. I make good judgments and choices in life.   **4 3 2 1**

3. I make good use of my time.   **4 3 2 1**

4. I enjoy other people.   **4 3 2 1**

5. I can succeed in goals that I really want to accomplish.   **4 3 2 1**

6. I am optimistic about the future.   **4 3 2 1**

7. I think for myself and defend my own beliefs and values.   **4 3 2 1**

8. I am a happy person most of the time.   **4 3 2 1**

Add up the numbers you circled. You should get a total score between 8 and 32.

Score:_____

Questionnaire 5 tells you how you generally feel about yourself and your abilities. It tells you what your overall self-confidence level is. If you have

- succeeded in school so far
- developed some special skills of your own, such as sports, music, and hobbies
- made a lot of friends over the years
- planned some career goals that you're following now

then you should be able to say to yourself, "I'm a winner. I believe in myself and I know I can succeed!"

If you do *not* feel good about yourself or about your abilities, your self-confidence may be low. Low self-confidence may be keeping you from doing the best you can. In this case, you need to change your feelings about yourself.

Look again at Questionnaire 5. This is what your score means:

Score

26-32 You have a very high level of general self-confidence.

20-25 Your general self-confidence is quite strong.

14-19 Your general self-confidence is satisfactory, but you might want to improve some aspects of your concept of yourself.

8-13 Your general self-confidence is quite low; you should think seriously about how to improve your view of yourself.

If your score was 20 to 32, you don't need to worry about your overall self-confidence; you feel very positive about yourself. If your score was between 8 and 19, ask yourself why you don't feel self-confident, and do something about it. See the exercises at the end of the chapter for some suggestions about what to do if your general self-confidence is low.

English-Specific Self-Confidence

Another kind of self-confidence is how you feel specifically about your ability in English. Are you confident when you speak English in class? Outside class? How do you feel about reading English? Writing English? Taking tests in English?

Your English-specific feelings may be a little different from your general feelings about yourself. Most people feel foolish when they make mistakes in a foreign language. Remember, your classmates will support you because they also make mistakes when they try to say and write things in English.

So if you feel bad about your English skills right now, it might be just because your *English-specific self-confidence* (how you feel about your English ability) is a little low. Don't let this bother you, especially if you have good general self-confidence. To improve your English-specific self-confidence, pay special attention to the *Speaking and Listening with a Partner* exercises at the end of this chapter.

Lowering Anxiety

One feeling that can stop you from having self-confidence is *anxiety*. Anxiety means that you are afraid of making mistakes because you feel your teacher will think you are stupid or your classmates will laugh at you.

Anxiety usually makes you feel overwhelmed by all the new material you have to learn. English may seem impossible to master. Therefore, you might have a hard time relaxing in your English class.

Many students of foreign languages feel anxious. A language is a very complex skill, and it takes a long time to learn one. If you have any feelings of anxiety, you are not alone.

How can your anxiety be lowered? Think about these strategies.

STRATEGIES FOR SUCCESS

1. **Develop overall self-confidence.**
   - Make a list of your strengths and weaknesses.
   - Set goals to overcome your weaknesses.
   - Tell yourself that you are smart and that you can do it.

2. **Think positively.**
   - Don't say "I can't" or "I'll never get it."
   - Don't let other classmates' bad attitudes affect you.
   - Respect your teacher and your teacher will respect you.

3. **Ask for help.**
   - Ask your teacher questions when you need to.
   - Ask your classmates for help when you need it.
   - Practice English as much as possible with your classmates.

As you try to lower your anxiety level, remember: foreign languages are difficult to learn, so you will probably always have a little anxiety in your English classes. Don't let a little anxiety discourage you. A few "butterflies in the stomach" can actually be helpful. Research shows that a little anxiety can be a positive feeling in many situations. Remember the last time you gave a presentation in class? You may have felt a little nervous before you began. That small nervousness was your body telling you that you were ready to do your best. So the next time you feel a little anxious, tell yourself it means that you're going to do a great job!

EXERCISES

Understanding Reading and Vocabulary

Here are some important words from this chapter:

confidence	anxiety
self-confidence	fear
optimistic	overwhelmed
specific	nervous

With a partner, do the following:

1. Define each word. Help each other out.
2. Check a dictionary if you have problems.
3. Use the words in sentences.

Speaking and Listening with a Partner

A. On your own, check any boxes for your skills that are *weak*. You may check more than one.

❑ Conversation

❑ Pronunciation

❑ Speaking in class

❑ Listening to conversations

❑ Listening to the teacher

❑ Reading academic textbooks

❑ Reading for pleasure (newspapers, magazines)

❑ Writing for academic purposes (research papers, etc.)

❑ Writing for pleasure

B. Put the skills you checked into the chart, one for each week.

Week 1 (this week's dates): _____

Skill: _____

Strategy: _____

Week 2 (dates): _____

Skill: _____

Strategy: _____

Week 3 (dates): _____

Skill: _____

Strategy: _____

C. With your partner, talk about some specific strategies you will use to improve your skills and write them in the chart on page 28.

Example

> Skill: _Reading for pleasure_
>
> Strategy: _Read five pages of an English novel or short story every day._

Discussing with the Whole Class

A. Look at the list of strategies for lowering anxiety on page 27. As a class, decide which three or four strategies are most important.

B. Write the important strategies on a Post-it and put it where you will see it every day.

Writing Your Journal

Look again at Questionnaire 5 on page 25. In your journal, do the following:

1. Choose two or three items on the questionnaire that you scored the _highest_ on, and write some things you do that are examples of them.

2. Pick two or three items on the questionnaire that you scored _lowest_ on, and list some goals for changing your general level of self-confidence for each item.

3. If your score was between 8 and 19, do you agree or disagree that your general self-confidence is low? Explain your answer in your journal.

6 Learning to Take Risks

speaking risk strategies listening success writing language understanding motivation reading culture goals

So far in this book you have studied the following topics:

- Your own learning styles and preferences
- Motivating yourself and setting your own goals
- How you can build self-confidence
- How to lower your anxiety

You have also learned to have some conversations in English and to read and write a little better in English. You are ready to learn to be a successful *risk taker*. Taking risks means you try to say things in English even if you might make a mistake. It's one of the most important strategies you can use. Let's look at why it's so important.

Language Ego

When you were growing up, you gradually began to understand yourself better. As an adult, you know what you like to do and what you don't like to do, what your strengths and weaknesses are, and what makes you special. This self that you have come to know well and to feel proud of is called your *ego*.

When you were about a year old, you began to speak your native language. Ever since then, you have been telling people what you know, what you think, and how you feel in your language. You have learned to understand yourself in your own language. Other people see you through your native language. This close connection between language and ego is called *language ego*: the way language helps you to understand and express yourself.

People get used to using their native language and seeing themselves through their native language. You are comfortable with the way you speak and understand others. Then you start to learn English: you do not speak fluently; you cannot say everything correctly; you don't understand everything. In English, you do not feel as intelligent, friendly, and charming as you feel in your native language. You can feel very frustrated as you try to speak in English. Why? Because your new language ego is weak.

Before you read further, do Questionnaire 6.

QUESTIONNAIRE 6   Language Ego

Circle the number that best describes you. Circle only one number for each item. Use the following scale:

1   *The sentence on the left describes you well.*

2   *The sentence on the left somewhat describes you.*

3   *The sentence on the right somewhat describes you.*

4   *The sentence on the right describes you well.*

Example

I don't care if people laugh at me.   1 **(2)** 3 **4**   I get very upset if people laugh a me.

Number 2 has been circled. This means that this person generally doesn't mind if people laugh at him or her.

---

1. I don't want to make mistakes because people will laugh at me.   **1 2 3 4**   Everyone makes mistakes, so it's okay to try out my English.

2. I must speak perfectly or no one will understand me.   **1 2 3 4**   Other people will not care if I make mistakes.

3. If my English is bad, I feel very stupid.   **1 2 3 4**   If my English is bad, I still have strong confidence in myself.

4. Classmates who speak English better than I do really bother me.   **1 2 3 4**   Classmates who are better than I am don't bother me.

5. A bad score on a test means that I am not intelligent.   **1 2 3 4**   A bad score on a test means that I need to study harder next time.

6. When my teacher corrects me, I feel ashamed.   **1 2 3 4**   When my teacher corrects me, I don't feel ashamed.

7. I hate making a fool of myself.   **1 2 3 4**   I don't mind making a fool of myself.

Add up the numbers you circled. You should get a total score between 7 and 28.

Score: _____

Questionnaire 6 tells you how strong your language ego is. This is what your score means:

Score

7-13	Weak language ego
14-21	Moderate language ego
22-28	Strong language ego

How did you score? If you have a weak or moderate language ego, you like to be safe when you use English. You like to be certain that what you are saying is correct. But research has shown that the most successful language learners take *risks*. They make guesses. They try out new things. They talk with others freely. How can you become more of a risk taker? Think about some of the ideas and strategies that follow.

Weak to Moderate Language Egos

A score of 7 to 21 means that you may feel somewhat afraid to speak English. You may be afraid that other people will think you are stupid. Or perhaps you think that because you don't speak English really well, other people will not like you. You probably do some of the following things:

- Sit near the back of the classroom.
- Speak only when you have to in your English class.
- Let other students talk most of the time in small group work.
- Don't try to speak English with other people outside class.
- Use very simple language that you know is grammatically correct.

To become a higher risk taker, remember to practice what you learned in Chapter 5. Try to increase your self-confidence and lower your anxiety. Then work on these strategies.

STRATEGIES FOR SUCCESS

1. Listen to English.
The first strategy is quite easy: *listen* to English as often as possible. When you just listen, you don't have to speak and risk making mistakes. Listen carefully in class, but also listen outside class on your own, as part of your homework. Watch English TV or go to a movie; listen to English radio programs and English songs.

2. Make opportunities to talk.
The second step in becoming a greater risk taker is to do lots of talking. It is important for you to speak English even if you make mistakes. You just have to risk saying things that aren't quite correct and be confident in yourself!

3. **Be willing to make mistakes.**
   You don't want to do anything that will make you look foolish or stupid because of your ego. You might feel that mistakes make you look weak and unintelligent. But to learn English successfully, you must tell yourself that *it's okay to make some mistakes.* Mistakes are not signs of weakness or failure. They are natural; everyone makes mistakes. So when you make a mistake, just keep talking and don't worry about it.

4. **Make your mistakes work for you.**
   When someone corrects you or tells you they don't understand you, try to remember your error. When people correct you, they are giving you useful information. For example, if you notice that people don't understand you when you use the /l/ and /r/ sounds in English, then you know you need to practice the sounds more. Make a list of errors you make. Try to notice them when you speak.

Strong Language Egos

If your score was 22 to 28, you are probably already a pretty good risk taker. You are not afraid of trying to use your English, and you don't mind too much if you make mistakes. You feel that mistakes are a natural part of learning, and if people correct you, you don't worry about it. You are quite confident in yourself and don't get anxious about speaking English.

Should you practice any strategies for better success? Here are some suggestions.

STRATEGIES FOR SUCCESS

1. **Make opportunities to use English outside the classroom.**
   You may feel quite confident about speaking English in the classroom, but do you make opportunities to use English outside the classroom? If not, make sure you listen to English and speak English with other people, not just your classmates and teacher. Watch English TV or go to a movie; listen to English radio programs and English songs. Find people who speak English; don't talk only with people who speak your native language.

2. **Make your mistakes work for you.**
   When someone corrects you or tells you they don't understand you, try to remember what your error was. When people correct you, they are giving you information about your English. For example, if you notice that people don't understand you when you use the /l/ and /r/ sounds in English, then you know you need to practice the sounds more. Make a list of errors you make. Try to notice them when you speak.

> **3. Take calculated risks.**
> While you are practicing English freely, don't forget to *think* a little bit about what you are going to say before you speak. Make sure your risks are calculated; that is, make sure you feel that most of the time your guesses about what you should say will be right. Don't make wild guesses that will be wrong most of the time. Try to be an *accurate* guesser.

One of my American friends told me about a time in Japan when she was eating with some friends in a restaurant. The food was really good, so she wanted to tell the waiter the food was great. She asked one of her friends how to say "great" in Japanese. Her friend gave her the word *oishi*, which actually means "delicious." You use the word to describe food. When the waiter came by, the American smiled, pointed to the food, and said, "Oishi." The waiter was very happy. Later in the evening at a nightclub, when a very handsome man finished a wonderful performance of a romantic song, she stood up and yelled out to him above the noise of the audience, "Oishi!" Everyone in the place laughed.

My friend was a risk taker. People laughed because the word *oishi* is never used for people or songs. But she learned something. She used the information people gave her and always used that word correctly after that.

EXERCISES

Understanding Reading and Vocabulary

Do the following three activities.

1. On your own, skim (quickly read) this chapter again in 5 minutes or less.
2. Write some notes about what the main ideas of the chapter are.
3. With a partner, tell each other what you think the main ideas were. Use your own words.

Speaking and Listening with a Partner

A. Look again at your score on Questionnaire 6 on page 31. Then look at the strategies that were suggested if your language ego is weak/moderate or strong. Write specific examples of things you can do to improve your score. Share them with your partner, and add your partner's ideas that you like.

B. Look at the following list of suggested strategies. Think of other strategies to add to the list. Then each choose *three* or *four* things to do right away this week. Write these strategies on Post-its. Put your list where you will see it every day.

Examples

Wherever you are

1. Use the Internet to get information in English.
2. Write an e-mail to someone in English.
3. Raise your hand in class to volunteer to speak.
4. Ask questions in class if you don't understand something.

If you are in an English-speaking country

1. With a partner and/or a classmate, eat lunch with native English speakers.
2. Start conversations with people while you're waiting in line for something.
3. Go to parties where people are speaking English.

If you are not in an English-speaking country

1. Go to places where you can find English speakers and talk with them.
2. Practice English with your classmates outside the classroom.
3. Buy and read an English language newspaper.

Discussing with the Whole Class

Write your Post-it strategies from the last exercise on the board for the rest of the class to see. If you like someone else's strategies, add them to your Post-its and use them.

Writing Your Journal

Answer these questions in your journal:

1. How well did the language ego questionnaire describe you? Give examples.
2. How do you feel when you make mistakes in front of your classmates?
3. Look back at all the Post-its you have been making. How well have you been following them? Highlight (with a colored marker) any strategies that you have not been doing, and write them in your journal now to remind you.

7 What's Your Language-Learning IQ?

Do you have to be intelligent to learn a foreign language? The answer is yes, but there are many different ways to define *intelligence*. Sometimes intelligence means that you are fast and accurate in taking tests. Sometimes intelligence is defined as being very smart in mathematics. Intelligence can also mean that you are very good at talking with people and understanding them.

For many people, intelligence means the mental abilities that are measured by an IQ (intelligence quotient) test. IQ tests are multiple-choice, timed tests kind of like the TOEFL. On IQ tests, you have to choose answers to word problems, mathematical problems, logic puzzles, and other questions very quickly. Your score on an IQ test supposedly tells you how smart you are.

Do you need to have a high score on an IQ test to be successful in English? According to experts, there are many different kinds of intelligence, and IQ tests measure only two types. There are at least five other kinds of intelligence as well. And those other types of intelligence might be more important for learning a language than IQ-test intelligence, depending on what kind of activity or task you are doing.

Which kinds of intelligence do you excel in? Before you read further, do Questionnaire 7.

QUESTIONNAIRE 7   Seven Kinds of Intelligence

Circle the number that best describes you. Circle only one number for each item. Use the following scale:

4   *Definitely, very much so!*

3   *Yes.*

2   *Not really.*

1   *Definitely not!*

Example

I like to learn by watching videos.   4 ③ 2 1

Number 3 has been circled. This means that this person agrees and thinks that this statement describes him or her well.

----

1. I like memorizing words.	4 3 2 1	
2. I like the teacher to explain grammar to me.	4 3 2 1	
3. I like making charts and diagrams.	4 3 2 1	
4. I like drama and role plays.	4 3 2 1	
5. I like singing songs in English.	4 3 2 1	
6. I like group and pair interaction.	4 3 2 1	
7. I like self-reflection through journal writing.	4 3 2 1	
8. I like word games and puzzles.	4 3 2 1	
9. I like problem-solving exercises.	4 3 2 1	
10. I like to learn through movies and videos.	4 3 2 1	
11. I like to move around a lot in the classroom.	4 3 2 1	
12. I like jazz chants and rhythmic activities.	4 3 2 1	
13. I like one-on-one conversation practice.	4 3 2 1	
14. I like to analyze my own performance.	4 3 2 1	

To figure out your score on Questionaire 7, see the directions for scoring that follow.

Add the numbers you circled on these *pairs* of items. You should get a total score between 2 and 8 for each pair.

Score

1. _____ + 8. _____ = _____ → linguistic intelligence
2. _____ + 9. _____ = _____ → logical–mathematical intelligence
3. _____ +10. _____ = _____ → spatial intelligence
4. _____ +11. _____ = _____ → bodily–kinesthetic intelligence
5. _____ +12. _____ = _____ → musical intelligence
6. _____ +13. _____ = _____ → interpersonal intelligence
7. _____ +14. _____ = _____ → intrapersonal intelligence

This is what your scores mean:

Score

7-8	Very high preference	**3-4**	Moderately low preference
5-6	Moderately high preference	**1-2**	Low preference

Questionnaire 7 tells you about the kinds of intelligence, that you prefer to use. Look at the following list of seven kinds of intelligence.

Linguistic intelligence	Speaking, using words, writing, communicating in a language, solving word problems
Logical–mathematical intelligence	Using numbers, logic, calculations; learning and understanding grammar rules
Spatial intelligence	Drawing, painting, using color, art, graphics, pictures, maps, and so on
Bodily–kinesthetic intelligence	Muscular coordination, athletic skill, body language, pronouncing a language
Musical intelligence	Using music, tones, hearing; producing the intonation and rhythm of a language
Interpersonal intelligence	Talking with other people, understanding them, using language to communicate well with other people
Intrapersonal intelligence	Self-knowledge, self-confidence, using language to analyze yourself

The first two, linguistic and logical–mathematical, are the types of intelligence measured on IQ tests. The other five are different kinds of intelligence, and maybe you will discover that some of them are important for learning a foreign language.

Which kinds of intelligence did you score highest on? Lowest? Your scores will give you an idea of what kinds of activities and tasks you prefer to do. Usually you like to do things that you do well, so your scores should tell you in which kinds of intelligence you are stronger than others.

What do your high scores and low scores mean? How will this information help you to learn English more successfully? Each kind of intelligence may be important, depending on the activity or task you are doing. If you are weak in some kinds of intelligence, then you need to become stronger in those areas to be a better language learner.

Look at the following chart. Find two or three kinds of intelligence you are weakest in. Then look at some things you can to do to become stronger in that area. The *Speaking and Listening with a Partner* exercise at the end of this chapter will help you to understand this chart even better.

STRATEGIES FOR SUCCESS

Kinds of Intelligence: Diagnostic Chart

If you are weak in . . .	then you should work hard on . . .
linguistic intelligence	understanding the teacher's explanations giving presentations reading English writing English learning word definitions
logical–mathematical intelligence	understanding grammar rules using grammar rules explaining grammar rules to others information gap exercises
spatial intelligence	using charts, diagrams, and maps using pictures/drawings seeing videos and movies
bodily–kinesthetic intelligence	pronunciation activities theater, drama hands-on projects body language, nonverbal communication
musical intelligence	pronunciation, intonation, rhythm, and stress singing songs, doing jazz chants
interpersonal intelligence	group and pair work talking with other students editing classmates' writing and speaking interviewing fluency activities
intrapersonal intelligence	independent study, self-assessment journal writing working on a computer

The most important lesson for you here is that you can make use of many different kinds of intelligence in learning English. Each of the seven kinds of intelligence is something you can be strong in. Continue to use your strengths in learning English. Strengthen the types you are weak in. The following exercises are activities to strengthen intelligence types.

EXERCISES

Understanding Reading and Vocabulary

With a partner, use some of the kinds of intelligence to study and practice vocabulary you don't know.

1. Scan the chapter for words you don't know. Write them in your notebook (linguistic intelligence).

2. Show your word list to your partner (interpersonal intelligence). Together, try to define the words by either acting them out (bodily–kinesthetic intelligence) or drawing pictures that show their meanings (spatial intelligence). If that isn't possible, give definitions of the words (linguistic intelligence).

3. Put the words on your list into groups that have related meanings (logical intelligence). For example, these words from page 36 are related: *accurate, smart, mental, ability, puzzle, logic.*

4. Make up a sentence that helps you to remember them: "The smart student had good mental ability, so he was accurate when answering questions with puzzles or logic."

5. Group them on a piece of paper according to their part of speech: Adjectives: *accurate, smart, mental;* Nouns: *ability, puzzle, logic.*

6. Finally, on your own, write the words down on index cards and then test yourself on their meanings (intrapersonal intelligence).

Speaking and Listening with a Partner

Look at your scores for Questionnaire 7 on page 38, and then look at the diagnostic chart on page 39. Talk about some specific strategies each of you could use to strengthen areas of intelligence. Put your strategies on a Post-it.

Discussing with the Whole Class

Divide the board into seven columns, one for each kind of intelligence. Write your Post-it strategies in the appropriate columns. After everyone has put their strategies on the board, choose a few of your classmates' strategies to write in your notebook. Use those strategies along with your original Post-it strategies.

Writing Your Journal

In your journal, answer these questions.

1. According to the questionnaire, which were your strongest two or three kinds of intelligence? Describe how you think those strengths help you to be successful in learning English.

2. Look at the goals you wrote down in Chapter 4. Have you reached those goals? How? If you have reached them, write some new goals. If you haven't reached your goals, write down specific things you need to do to accomplish them.

8 The Influence of Your Native Language

I WONDER IF THEY WILL BE STUDYING FOR OUR 考試 TOMORROW.

Think of someone from another country trying to speak your native language. You usually know where this person comes from because of his or her *accent*. Native speakers of English are often quickly identified because of the way they speak. Sometimes they sound a little strange or even funny.

We can usually recognize foreign accents because the sounds of our native language are different from those of a foreign language. We can also recognize typical grammar mistakes when we hear someone speaking our native language. Think about your native language and the parts of English that are hard for you. They are probably hard because those sounds or patterns are very different from, or don't exist in, your native language. These are some examples:

- If your native language is Japanese or Korean, the difference between /l/ and /r/ in English (as in *low* and *glass* vs. *row* and *grass*) may be difficult to pronounce.
- If your native language is Spanish or Thai, it may be difficult to pronounce the English sounds /b/ and /v/ (as in *bent* and *berry* vs. *vent* and *very*).
- If your native language is French, it may be a little difficult to use the present perfect tense (*I have lived here since January*) because in French you just use the present.

It's natural for native English speakers to know what your native language is when you speak English. Your accent and grammar are probably typical of people from your country. Very few nonnative English speakers ever develop absolutely perfect accents. Unless you learned English as a very young child, you will probably not sound exactly like a native speaker of English.

Before you read further, do Questionnaire 8.

QUESTIONNAIRE 8   Pronunciation

Circle the number that best describes your English ability right now. Circle only one number for each item. Use the following scale:

4   *I'm really good here; I do not need to work on this any more.*

3   *I'm okay here, but I could work a little on this.*

2   *I'm not so good here and need to work on this quite a bit.*

1   *I'm very bad here and need lots of work on this.*

Example

Playing the piano   **4 3 2 ①**

Number 1 has been circled. This means that this person's piano playing is terrible.

----

1. Pronouncing the words *seat* and *sit*   **4 3 2 1**

2. Pronouncing the words *sit* and *set*   **4 3 2 1**

3. Pronouncing the words *set* and *sat*   **4 3 2 1**

4. Pronouncing the words *not* and *note*   **4 3 2 1**

5. Pronouncing the words *look* and *Luke*   **4 3 2 1**

6. Pronouncing the words *nut* and *not*   **4 3 2 1**

7. Pronouncing words with *l* in them (*glass, low, yellow*)   **4 3 2 1**

8. Pronouncing words with *r* in them (*grass, row, arrow*)   **4 3 2 1**

9. Pronouncing words with voiced *th* in them (*this, other*)   **4 3 2 1**

10. Pronouncing words with unvoiced *th* in them (*thin, author*) **4 3 2 1**

11. Pronouncing words with *b* in them (*berry, labor*)   **4 3 2 1**

12. Pronouncing words with *v* in them (*very, ever*)   **4 3 2 1**

13. Pronouncing words with *f* in them (*far, offer, if*)   **4 3 2 1**

14. Putting the correct stress on words like *information, proficiency, capitalize, interesting*   **4 3 2 1**

15. Giving correct intonation to questions like *Are you sure?*   **4 3 2 1**

16. Giving correct intonation to questions like *Where is he?*   **4 3 2 1**

Add up the numbers you circled. You should get a total score between 16 and 64.

Score: _____

Questionnaire 8 may remind you of a few sounds in English that are still difficult for you. This is what your score means:

Score

55-64   Your pronunciation is great! You only have a few sounds in English to work on.

45-54   Your pronunciation is good, but you have several areas that you still need to work on.

35-44   Your pronunciation is okay, but work on the items with lower scores.

Below 35   You should work on many areas of pronunciation.

Of course, remember that you rated *yourself* on this questionnaire. You may have been too hard or too easy on yourself. Nevertheless, the questionnaire might help you to identify some specific problem sounds in English that you need to work extra hard on.

Why are some sounds more difficult than others? Usually, the most difficult sounds are the ones that your native language does not have. You use your knowledge of your native language to learn English. If your native language is Japanese, you might say *grass* when you really mean *glass*. If your native language is Thai, you might say *werry* when you really want to say *very*. It's a simple process, but it can be difficult sometimes to retrain the mouth muscles you developed speaking your native language.

Applying what you already know is a natural process any time you learn anything. For example, if you're just learning to ski, you use previous experiences and knowledge to learn this new skill. On a pair of skis, as you try to keep your balance, make turns, control your speed, and most important, stop, you remember things like running down a hill, sliding on a slide, and walking on a slippery sidewalk. You use those memories to help you to learn to ski.

How important is your accent? Is it bad if people know your native language when you speak English? First, very few adult learners of foreign languages ever sound like native speakers; it's natural for you to have an accent. Second, your accent is a reflection of who you are, and you should be proud of your background. Third, your goal should be to say things *clearly* so that others understand you, not to worry about pronunciation that is not perfect.

STRATEGIES FOR SUCCESS

Try the following steps to improve your accent in English.

1. **Listen carefully to native English speakers.**
   You can help yourself a lot by listening to other people and listening specifically for certain sounds. Pick out certain sounds or sound patterns, and then keep repeating them to yourself. Listen to radio and TV and focus on specific sounds you need to work on.

2. **Listen to yourself carefully.**
   Whenever you speak English, notice the sounds of the language, and the stress and intonation patterns. Choose certain sounds or sound patterns that are difficult for you and focus on those. Read aloud just to practice pronouncing English. Record yourself on a tape recorder and then listen to yourself. Keep recording yourself until you improve.

3. **Speak English without worrying about what you sound like.**
   You may feel embarrassed. That's a natural feeling. But most people will be kind to you when you speak English, so don't worry too much about making pronunciation mistakes.

What about the grammar of English: verbs, word order, prepositions, articles, words, idioms, and all that? Here, too, your native language influences you. How do you avoid the comfortable native language habits?

STRATEGIES FOR SUCCESS

1. **Don't do a lot of translating to or from your native language.**
   Don't always think of a native language translation for words or phrases. Just try to understand them in English. Get into the habit of thinking directly in English.

2. **Use your native language intuitions as you speak English.**
   Sometimes you will find that your native language actually helps you. Many English words come from some other language, maybe your own. And your native language may have borrowed many English words. Even some English grammar rules may be similar to those in your language.

3. **Use your mistakes as learning opportunities.**
   You can make your mistakes work for you, rather than against you. Notice the grammar mistakes you make, write them down on a piece of paper, and repeat the correct forms to yourself. Try to self-correct while you are still talking, then try the correct grammar the next time it comes up in a conversation.

4. **Be more childlike.**
   Children can teach you a lesson on how to learn English. They like to move *directly* into a foreign language. They don't think about their native language when they have a conversation. They don't translate things as they're listening or speaking. Your best strategy would be to try being a little more childlike.

EXERCISES

Understanding Reading and Vocabulary

With a partner, look at these sentences. Without looking in your dictionary, decide what the underlined word or phrase means.

1. We're usually quite good at <u>recognizing</u> foreign accents.
2. Your accent and grammar are probably <u>typical</u> of people from your country.
3. It's sometimes very difficult to overcome the <u>influence</u> of your native language.
4. Your accent is a <u>reflection</u> of who you are, so you should be proud of your background.
5. You find it hard to <u>get rid of</u> the habits of your native language and to get used to other ways of saying things.
6. Your native language may have <u>borrowed</u> many English words.

Speaking and Listening with a Partner

Look at Questionnaire 8 on page 43. Find the five or six items that are most difficult for you. Use your answers to make a schedule of goals for the next few weeks. Write your schedule in your notebook. Write the goals for each week and possible times to work on your weak points. Your schedule might look like this.

Week 1	Before school	/l/ and /r/ distinction (*light* vs. *right*, etc.)
Week 2	After school	Present perfect tense (I *have seen* that movie.)
Week 3	On the bus	/i/ and /I/ distinction (*beat* vs. *bit*)

Then talk with your partner about specific strategies you can use to practice the goals you have written.

Discussing with the Whole Class

On pages 44–45, you found strategies for improving your pronunciation and grammar. Share with the rest of the class things you have already done to improve pronunciation or grammar and things you can do in the future. Take notes on what other students say.

Writing Your Journal

In your journal, answer these questions.

1. What strategies did other students talk about in the last exercise about improving their pronunciation or grammar?
2. What specific strategies did you and your partner talk about using to practice your goals in the *Speaking and Listening with a Partner* exercise?

9 Learning a Second Culture

Learning a second language always means learning a second culture. Language and culture are connected. When you greet someone or say no to an invitation or talk with people in an informal conversation—all these situations are cultural. Culture is a set of guidelines for communicating with other people, rules for being polite or formal, and customs or ways of doing things.

Think about people who try to learn the language and culture of your country. What are some of the differences between your culture and theirs? What kinds of difficulties do they have? They probably have to learn about such things as:

Food	Shopping, restaurants, menus, and ordering
Transportation	Trains and buses and how to use them
Work	What to say and do while working
Time	Being on time, keeping appointments
Entertainment	Songs, TV shows, movies, theater
Health	Getting medical advice, talking to a doctor
Dress	Clothes that are correct for different occasions
Respect for others	Showing proper respect
Friends	Making friends

This list could continue. If you want to participate in these aspects of culture, you must be able to speak the language of the culture. Even if you never go to an English-speaking country, you still need to learn culture because some day you may need to speak or write to someone from an English-speaking culture. This chapter will help you to develop some strategies for understanding culture.

Before you read further, do Questionnaire 9.

QUESTIONNAIRE 9   Cultural Differences

For all the items on this questionnaire, refer to your own country, labeled here as "My Country" (MC), and to an "English-speaking Country" (ESC) of your choice. Write the names of the two countries:

MC: _____   ESC: _____

In each of the questionnaire items, circle the number that best describes your country (MC) and the number that best describes the English-speaking country (ESC).

Example

BASEBALL   **Difference Score**

MC: Popular   4   3 ② 1   Not popular

ESC: Popular   ④ 3   2   1   Not popular   2

Number 2 has been circled for "My Country" (MC) and number 4 for "English speaking Country" (ESC). This means that this person thinks that baseball is not so popular in his or her country but very popular in the English-speaking country. The larger number (4) minus the smaller number (2) equals the cultural difference score (2).

Difference Score

1. TRAINS

    MC: Efficient   4   3   2   1   Not efficient

    ESC: Efficient   4   3   2   1   Not efficient   _____

2. SMOKING

    MC: Many do it   4   3   2   1   Few do it

    ESC: Many do it   4   3   2   1   Few do it   _____

3. DIVORCE

    MC: Not acceptable   4   3   2   1   Acceptable

    ESC: Not acceptable   4   3   2   1   Acceptable   _____

4. HAMBURGERS

    MC: Not popular   4   3   2   1   Popular

    ESC: Not popular   4   3   2   1   Popular   _____

Difference Score

5. GRANDPARENTS

 MC: Respected   **4 3 2 1**   Not respected

 ESC: Respected   **4 3 2 1**   Not respected   _____

6. FAMILIES

 MC: Many children   **4 3 2 1**   Few children

 ESC: Many children   **4 3 2 1**   Few children   _____

7. PARENTS

 MC: Important   **4 3 2 1**   Not important

 ESC: Important   **4 3 2 1**   Not important   _____

8. SOCIETY

 MC: Friendly to strangers   **4 3 2 1**   Not friendly

 ESC: Friendly to strangers   **4 3 2 1**   Not friendly   _____

9. PEOPLE

 MC: Look alike   **4 3 2 1**   Many different kinds

 ESC: Look alike   **4 3 2 1**   Many different kinds   _____

10. WORKERS

 MC: Hard-working   **4 3 2 1**   Relaxed and easy-going

 ESC: Hard-working   **4 3 2 1**   Relaxed and easy-going   _____

Add up the numbers in the right column. You should have a total score between 0 and 30

Score: _____

Questionnaire 9 tells you how different you think your culture is from the culture of the English-speaking country. Your total is your cultural difference score. This is what your score means:

Score
- **0-10** Very few differences
- **11-20** Moderate differences
- **21-30** Great differences

Remember, these are your own views and ideas about the two cultures. They are very important because they are your feelings.

If your score is between 0 and 10, enjoy the similarities you see, but don't forget to be curious about the differences and enjoy them, too. If your score is between 11 and 20 or 21 and 30, it's important to find out as much as you can about the culture of this English-speaking country. Because you see it as different from your own, you have exciting opportunities to discover new things and to learn about a new and different culture.

Understanding Another Culture

To improve your English, try to understand the culture of an English-speaking country. When you see differences, ask people about them, read about them, and learn about them. Use your English to find answers to your questions about the culture. Enjoy the differences.

However, be careful, because sometimes what you *think* is true about a group of people is not. For example, not all North Americans are friendly, have a lot of money, live in big houses, and look like Keanu Reeves or Meg Ryan. North Americans can sometimes be unfriendly, poor, live in small, crowded apartments, and look like Asians, South Americans, or Africans.

What do people from other countries think about people in your country? Do they think you all look alike or live in the same kind of houses? With your English, you can tell people about culture in your country, too.

Do you know the English expression "put yourself in someone else's shoes"? It means "try to understand another culture by becoming a part of the culture." If you are now living in an English-speaking country, you have a perfect opportunity to put your feet in different shoes. You can learn something interesting about native English speakers and practice your English at the same time.

If you're not living in an English-speaking country, you still have an opportunity to learn as much as you can about English-speaking cultures. With your English skills you can read, watch television, and talk to people from other countries in English.

Culture Shock

As you were growing up, you used your native language for everything. Your native language ego (see Chapter 6) was strong. You became comfortable using your native language.

Now that you have begun to learn English, your language ego in English is probably not very strong yet. One reason for this is that your English is still limited. If you are living in an English-speaking country, an additional reason for a weaker language ego is that you are not yet used to the new culture. You may be experiencing *culture shock*. Culture shock is a feeling of confusion about what to say and do in a new and different culture. You feel frustrated about your ability to say the right thing, and maybe you even think people are laughing at you for being foreign. You might feel a little homesick and want to return to your own country.

Most people have culture shock for a few months or even a year after they move to a new country and have to speak a new language. So if you are now in an English-speaking country and have been there only a short time, don't worry. Follow these suggestions and your culture shock will probably decrease.

STRATEGIES FOR SUCCESS

1. Find things to enjoy: movies, TV, sports, restaurants, books, and so on.

2. Make friends with as many local people as possible.

3. Ask questions when you don't understand something about local culture.

4. Try to think positively about your new culture.

5. Remember, no place is perfect, including your country.

6. Don't be upset: Culture shock is normal and you'll get over it.

EXERCISES

Understanding Reading and Vocabulary

Skim through this chapter and write five comprehension questions about the chapter. Then work with a partner and ask each other the questions.

Example

A: What does *culture* mean?
B: It means customs or ways of doing things.

Speaking and Listening with a Partner

A. Make two columns in your notebook. Write the name of your country in the first column and the name of an English-speaking country—such as the United States, Canada, or Australia—in the second column. Then, with a partner, brainstorm words or phrases that describe people from your country and from an English-speaking country that you both know. List the words in the columns.

Example

My Country	English-speaking Country
polite	friendly
religious	loud
on time	stressed

Try to think of five to ten words or phrases for each list.

B. Ask each other this question: Are these words/phrases true for *all* people from your country and *all* people from the other country? Explain your answers to each other.

Discussing with the Whole Class

A. Divide into groups of four. Tell your group some experiences you have had with culture shock. Describe examples of what you felt. If you were able to overcome your feelings, tell the group what you did to do so. Compare what classmates say with the list on page 51.

B. Share your group's ideas with the class. Write down in your notebook any new ideas that other groups suggested.

Writing Your Journal

A. Plan some strategies for using English through understanding differences between your culture and an English-speaking culture. For example, you might:

1. List three to five positive things about the English-speaking country.
2. List different ways for you to use your English more with local people (include speaking, listening, reading, and writing).
3. Write questions about the new culture that you would like to ask someone.

B. Answer this question: When you speak English, do you feel that your personality changes a little? Do you feel as if you are different when you speak English? If so, describe your feelings.

10 Using Individual Learning Strategies

So far in this book, you have learned and practiced strategies to help you to

- Understand your own learning styles
- Use both right-brain and left-brain processing
- Plan your own goals
- Improve your self-confidence
- Lower your anxiety
- Take risks
- Use several different kinds of intelligence
- Recognize the influence of your native language
- Learn a second culture along with your second language.

Some of these strategies are easy to do on your own, without help from other people. For other strategies you need help. This chapter focuses on some *individual* learning strategies. Although we use language to communicate with other people, some of your English learning can be done on your own, away from classmates, friends, and teachers.

Before reading further, do Questionnaire 10.

QUESTIONNAIRE 10 The Individual Learner

Circle the number that best describes how often you do these activities in English. Circle only one number. Use the following scale:

5   *Always*

4   *Often*

3   *Sometimes*

2   *Seldom*

1   *Never*

Example

Play tennis   5 4 3 ②1

Number 2 has been circled. This means that this person seldom plays tennis.

----

1. Watch television, listen to radio, and so on (news, other programs)	5 4 3 2 1
2. Watch movies, plays, and so on	5 4 3 2 1
3. Listen to other people's conversations	5 4 3 2 1
4. Listen for specific sounds in English when people speak to me	5 4 3 2 1
5. Listen for specific grammar points (verb tenses, articles, and so on)	5 4 3 2 1
6. Practice conversations by myself	5 4 3 2 1
7. Repeat language from an audiotape	5 4 3 2 1
8. Practice pronunciation of specific sounds	5 4 3 2 1
9. Read aloud	5 4 3 2 1
10. Skim for the overall topic and message before reading	5 4 3 2 1
11. Scan a passage quickly to find specific information	5 4 3 2 1
12. Figure out the meaning of an unclear passage	5 4 3 2 1
13. Guess meanings of words from the context	5 4 3 2 1
14. Freewrite on my own (diary, journal, e-mail)	5 4 3 2 1
15. Write several drafts of an academic paper	5 4 3 2 1
16. Proofread my written work	5 4 3 2 1

Add up the numbers you circled. You should have a total score between 16 and 80.

Score: _____

Questionnaire 10 tells you how often you use strategies that you can do by yourself. This is what your score means:

Score

16-35   You seldom use individual strategies.

36-63   You sometimes use individual strategies.

64-80   You often use individual strategies.

How did you score? If your score was 63 or below, you probably could make more progress in English if you practiced more often on your own. This takes extra time and extra effort. But to learn English well, you need to work hard outside your classroom. A few extra minutes every now and then may make a big difference. You just have to plan to do something specific almost every day.

Here are some stories about language learners who were successful because they practiced strategies on their own.

Successful Individual Learners

Leonard Bernstein, the famous American musician and conductor, was also a successful language learner. When he visited a new country, he tried to learn some of the language of that country. Here is what he did: (1) Before the trip, Bernstein learned simple vocabulary and phrases. He spent about forty hours by himself with a dictionary and a phrase book and memorized useful words like *hotel, room, bathroom, menu, How much? Where is* _____? (2) Then, Bernstein worked with a conversation partner practicing the language, but after each session, he practiced alone, repeating the things he had learned with his conversation partner.

As a young boy of about fourteen, Hans Durbeek, from Holland, invented little conversations in English as he walked to and from school. In other words, he pretended he was talking with someone in English. He practiced like this every day and became the best English speaker in his school.

A few years ago, before I went to Yugoslavia, I tried to learn some Serbo-Croatian. For about a month before I went, every day I listened to tapes in my car and repeated words and phrases. When I got there, I tried to use my memorized phrases as often as possible. The result was that I talked a little bit with people and had fun doing it!

There are many strategies you can do on your own to improve your English. Here are some suggestions.

STRATEGIES FOR SUCCESS

1. The Internet

The Internet is an amazing source for language practice. Today, about 80 percent of all World Wide Web (www) sites around the world are in English, so wherever you are, if you have a computer, you can easily find English on the Internet. Here are some suggestions for individual English practice on the Internet.

- **Activities and exercises.** Many publishers and language schools around the world have their own Web sites that offer various activities and exercises in English. For example, www.eslcafe.com and www.longman.com offer many different opportunities to practice English. There are also Web sites that offer English courses on line, such as www.EnglishSuccess.com. These sites have many different types of courses. Many of these courses are taught by an English teacher who grades your progress from anywhere around the world after you register and pay for a course. One good thing about on-line courses is that you can study whenever you want to and for as long or as short a time as you want to.

- **E-mail.** If you do not have an e-mail account, now is the time to get one so that you can communicate with people around the world in English. Several e-mail servers are free: www.hotmail.com, for example, offers a free e-mail account. To find e-mail "pen pals", log onto a site such as Dave's ESL cafe (www.eslcafe.com) and you will find lists of people you can "talk" to by e-mail.

- **Information.** Would you like information about another country? a topic of current interest? a famous actor or actress? today's newspaper in English? Again, using a convenient search engine (such as www.yahoo.com), type in two or three keywords and you will almost immediately find many different Web sites to choose from. Read through them, take notes, follow up on related Web sites, and learn—all in English.

- **Shopping.** People claim that there is nothing you cannot shop for on the Internet, so here's a chance to use English and to look for things you might want to buy. Of course, you don't have to buy anything, you can just look! Use a search engine such as www.yahoo.com and type in the name of your favorite store(s) and you will quickly be able to find their on-line catalog. Be sure it's in English, because you want to practice English!

2. Songs

Another way to practice English is to sing English songs. Listen to the radio, play CDs or cassettes, and sing along in English. It will help your pronunciation while you have some fun.

3. Poetry

Have you ever tried to write a simple poem in English? Your grammar doesn't have to be perfect in poetry, so it's easy to write. You don't even have to make every line rhyme. Try it! Your reward will be some interesting and possibly beautiful thoughts in English. A student once wrote a poem about a poor person sitting on a bench in a park with leaves all over the ground. Here is the poem. Notice that the grammar is not perfect, but the feelings are quite clear.

*One day in the morning
  it was hot continue one month ago.*

*Look at everywhere with sad,
  the leaves fall down when the wind blow.*

*On the floor full of leaves
  side by side everywhere.*

*Anything was confusion,
  look like somebody*

*Was to trouble by poorness
  of mankind.*

4. Word categories

When you learn vocabulary, try putting words into categories in English. For example, write down words that rhyme, such as *possession*, *obsession*, *regression*. Or write lists of words that start with the same letter, like *possession*, *powerful*, *potential*. You can make index cards with these words on them so you can practice them later.

5. Crossword puzzles

Do you like crossword puzzles? They can help you to learn English words. Look in an English newspaper, or on the Internet, search for the keywords *crossword puzzle*, and you will see several possibilities for downloading crossword puzzles that are at your level. Other word games in English are helpful, too. *Boggle* is a game with letters on dice with which you have to make words; you can play this game alone. You can also buy magazines with word puzzles in them.

EXERCISES

Understanding Reading and Vocabulary

A. Look again at Questionnaire 10 on page 54. There are some important words listed in the two categories on reading and writing. Find the meaning of the following words, from a partner or a dictionary, and write their definitions in your notebook. (Each word is a strategy.)

draft (of a paper) freewrite proofread scan skim

B. With your partner, talk about your next opportunity to use each of the five strategies. For example, if your teacher has assigned an essay, try freewriting on the topic first, then writing several drafts of the paper, then finally proofreading it carefully.

Speaking and Listening with a Partner

A. Look at the Internet strategies listed on page 56. Share with your partner any experience you already have in searching for things on the Internet.

B. Work together on a computer or in a computer lab, and begin some of the searches that are suggested. Decide which Web sites are the most interesting or useful. Write down the Web site addresses. Later, you can log on to the Web sites on your own and practice your English.

Discussing with the Whole Class

Look at the poetry strategy in the list of strategies on pages 56–57. In a small group, write some poetry together. Here is a simple structure for you to follow.

Line 1:   Noun (or noun phrase)

Line 2:   Three adjectives

Line 3:   A verb phrase in the *-ing* form

Line 4:   A verb phrase in the *-ing* form

Line 4:   One adjective

Here is an example.

Mount Shasta

Gigantic, beautiful, powerful

Spreading across the land

Filling the sky

Awesome

Write several poems if you have time. Then, on the board write the poem your group thinks is the best one and read it to the rest of the class. If you don't understand a word you see on the board, ask what it means.

Writing Your Journal

A. Choose one of the four skills in Questionnaire 10 (listening, speaking, reading, or writing) on which you spend the *most* time. Write about several specific things you do to practice the skill.

Example

Listening: When I ride the bus alone, I listen to other people's conversations and try to understand them.

B. Choose the skill on which you spend the *least* amount of time. Write about several things you could do to improve your strategy use in that category. Be specific!

Example

Speaking: I will talk to my neighbor every time I see her and ask her questions.

List the strategies on a Post-it and use them in the next few weeks.

11 | Using Group Strategies

Language is used for communication. It is a way to understand other people's thoughts, feelings, and ideas. With language you can tell others about your own thoughts, feelings, and ideas. Therefore, a large amount of your English language practice should involve other people. Some practice of English can be done individually, as you saw in the last chapter, but *communication* practice must be done with other people.

In this chapter we talk about two characteristics of communication and interaction with other people: *extroversion* and *introversion*.

Before you read further, do Questionnaire 11.

QUESTIONNAIRE 11 Extroversion and Introversion

Circle the letter that best describes you.

Example

In the classroom, I

(**a.**) ask the teacher a lot of questions.

b. hardly ever ask the teacher a question.

*Letter **a** has been circled. This means that this person asks the teacher a lot of questions.*

----

1. I usually like
   a. working with other people.
   b. working alone.

2. I'm
   a. easy for people to talk with.
   b. somewhat shy.

3. I'm happiest when I'm
   a. with other people.
   b. alone.

4. At a party, I
   a. start conversations with people I don't know.
   b. wait for someone to talk with me.

5. I solve problems better by
   a. talking with others about it.
   b. analyzing them on my own.

6. In my free time, I prefer
   a. to go out with other people.
   b. to stay at home by myself.

7. Talking with people I don't know
   a. is interesting and exciting.
   b. is difficult and makes me tired.

8. When I'm by myself I usually feel
   a. lonely and anxious.
   b. peaceful and calm.

9. In a classroom I prefer
   a. group work with other students.
   b. individual work on my own.

Add up only the "a" answers you circled. You should get a total score between 0 and 9.

Score: ____

Questionnaire 11 tells you if you are usually *extroverted* or *introverted* in your feelings and activities. If you're extroverted, you're outgoing and want other people around you. If you're introverted, you're shy and prefer being alone.

This is what your score means:

Score

8-9	Very extroverted
6-7	Somewhat extroverted
3-5	Somewhat introverted
0-2	Very introverted

If your score was between 6 and 9, you enjoy working and talking with other people and you like to have other people around you. You're probably naturally extroverted, so communicating with other people isn't difficult. In your English class, you usually see your classmates and your teacher as partners or members of your team. Extroversion can be useful for learning a language.

On the other hand, if your score was between 0 and 5, you enjoy being alone, are a little anxious when you have to talk with strangers, and are quite comfortable finding solutions to problems on your own. You'll need to work a little harder to use English with other people, including your classmates. The purpose of language is communication, so you should try to relax when you are talking with others.

Both extroversion and introversion have advantages and disadvantages. One is not better than the other. Extroverts like to be around other people. They feel more comfortable when other people are around and dislike being alone. Extroverts do not always talk a lot; they usually just like to be with other people.

Introverts don't need other people as much and prefer to be on their own. Sometimes introverts are a little shy and afraid to take risks in communication.

Look at the following chart, which shows advantages and disadvantages of extroversion and introversion.

	Extrovert	**Introvert**
Advantages	• Practicing English with other people is natural and easy for you. • You usually don't mind taking risks. • You enjoy group work in class.	• You enjoy solving problems on your own. • You are happy by yourself. • You usually have good study skills.
Disadvantages	• You can be too dependent on people. • You might not study enough on your own. • You don't like individual work.	• You might not try to meet other people. • You could be a low risk taker. • You don't like group work.

The important thing is to know yourself well and to use strategies to help yourself to become a more successful learner.

STRATEGIES FOR SUCCESS

If you are extroverted:
- Continue to practice your English with other people.
- Continue to talk with your classmates when you do group work in class.
- Try to study on your own a little more.
- Focus a little more on practicing your English by yourself.

If you are introverted:
- Continue to study on your own.
- Continue to practice English by yourself.
- Try to practice your English with other people a little more.
- Try to talk more with your classmates when you do group work in class.

One of the most important characteristics of language is its use in interacting with other people. When you speak and listen, and also when you read and write, you are interacting with someone else. The best way to interact with other people is to think of your classmates, your teacher, and other people as members of your team. You can all help each other to learn English. This means that you do not look at others, especially your classmates, as people who are competing with you; you are all trying together to learn English.

Try these strategies for interacting with your classmates.

STRATEGIES FOR SUCCESS

1. **Interact with your classmates.**
   - Ask your classmates questions when you don't understand something.
   - Give answers when your classmates ask you something; participate happily in group work, partner work, and discussions.
   - Try to understand your classmates.
   - Consider your classmates as members of your own "team."

2. **Cooperate with your teacher.**
   - Listen carefully to directions your teacher gives in class.
   - Pay special attention to directions for group and partner activities.
   - Understand what your role is in group/partner work.
   - Ask your teacher if you don't understand something.

> **3. Communicate with speakers of English.**
> - Find situations where you can talk with other English speakers outside your classroom.
> - Ask others to repeat, explain, slow down, or give examples if you don't understand them.
> - Ask for help from others when you cannot say something correctly in English.
> - Be happy when other people give you feedback.

For all these interactive strategies, you need to be somewhat extroverted. By using the strategies you should become more cooperative and be able to use English more successfully.

EXERCISES

Understanding Reading and Vocabulary

Check your comprehension of this chapter with this true-false quiz. Write **T** if the statement is true, **F** if the statement is false.

1. _____ Most practice in English should be done alone, on your own.

2. _____ Extroverted people feel happiest when they are with others.

3. _____ Introverted people are not very strong because they are lonely.

4. _____ Extroverts are more cooperative than introverts because they enjoy other people.

5. _____ Extroverts are better language learners than introverts because they are talkative.

6. _____ Both extroverts and introverts can benefit from using new strategies.

7. _____ It's important to compete with your classmates.

The answers are on page 65.

Speaking and Listening with a Partner

Look at the sections on pages 63–64 that list ways to become a more interactive learner. Choose two or three strategies and discuss specifically what you will do to practice them. Write them on a Post-it to help you remember them.

Discussing with the Whole Class

Share your strategies on the Post-it, from the *Listening and Speaking with a Partner* exercise, with the rest of the class. Write your strategies on the board. As your classmates write their strategies, write any new ideas in your notebook that you would like to practice.

Writing Your Journal

Answer the following questions.

1. How well did the questionnaire describe you? Explain.
2. Look at the chart on page 62 that shows advantages and disadvantages of extroversion and introversion. Make a list of specific strategies you can use to overcome any disadvantages you have in your introversion/extroversion style. Copy that list onto a Post-it, put it where you will see it, and practice those strategies this week.

Answers to the true-false quiz in the *Understanding Reading and Vocabulary* exercise: 1. F, 2. T, 3. F, 4. F, 5. F, 6. T, 7. F

12 Strategies for Taking Tests

Tests are a part of almost every class you take in school. Sometimes tests are given at the beginning of a course to help the teacher discover what you know and don't know. Other types of tests, such as quizzes, weekly tests, and midterm tests, are given during the course to measure your progress. A final examination is often given at the end of a course. Another category of test is a general proficiency test, like the TOEFL, TOEIC, and college entrance examinations.

How good a test taker are you? Do you prepare well for tests? Do you take enough time to review material? Do you stay confident that you will do well on a test? Or are you often anxious and lacking in self-confidence? If so, how does your anxiety affect your test score? If you are a good test taker, then you may only need to quickly review the strategies in this chapter. If you are not a good test taker, you can help yourself by following some of the strategies here.

In this chapter, we first take a look at general strategies for taking *classroom tests*. Then we look briefly at some hints for taking *standardized tests*.

Before you read further, do Questionnaire 12.

QUESTIONNAIRE 12 Classroom Tests

Each of the following items refers to classroom tests that you have taken.
Circle the number that best describes you. Use the following scale:

5 *I always do this.*

4 *I often do this.*

3 *I sometimes do this.*

2 *I seldom do this.*

1 *I never do this.*

Example

Before a test

I mark my calendar with the date of the test.   5 ④ 3 2 1

Number 4 has been circled. This means that this person often marks his or her calendar with the date of the test.

Before a test

1. I discover everything I can about the test.   5 4 3 2 1

2. I create a plan for review.   5 4 3 2 1

3. I review the material thoroughly.   5 4 3 2 1

4. I take practice tests or do practice exercises.   5 4 3 2 1

5. I review with a group of classmates.   5 4 3 2 1

6. I tell myself to relax and feel confident.   5 4 3 2 1

7. I get a good night's sleep.   5 4 3 2 1

During the test

1. I arrive at the classroom early.   5 4 3 2 1

2. I quickly look over the whole test before answering anything.   5 4 3 2 1

3. I estimate how much time each part of the test will take before answering anything.   5 4 3 2 1

4. I concentrate very carefully.   5 4 3 2 1

5. I leave enough time at the end to check all my answers.   5 4 3 2 1

After the test

1. I think of the test as an opportunity to learn something.   **5 4 3 2 1**

2. I look up questions that I think I might have missed.   **5 4 3 2 1**

3. I pay attention to my teacher's feedback on the test.   **5 4 3 2 1**

4. I use this test experience to be better prepared for the next test.   **5 4 3 2 1**

Add up the numbers you circled. You should get a total score between 16 and 80.

Score: ＿＿＿

Questionnaire 12 tells you how good a classroom test taker you are. This is what your score means:

Score

16-32	Low use of test-taking strategies
33-48	Average use of test-taking strategies
49-64	Moderately high use of test-taking strategies
65-80	High use of test-taking strategies

If you scored 16 to 48, you should improve your habits for preparing for and taking classroom tests. If you scored between 49 and 64, you are using quite a few good strategies, and you are probably a good test taker, but you can still improve. If you scored in the 65 to 80 category, congratulations on being a very good test-taker! Perhaps you can help a classmate to become better.

Before the Classroom Test

Preparation for tests is necessary to perform well. Here are some suggestions to help you prepare for a test.

STRATEGIES FOR SUCCESS

1. **Discover everything you can about the test you are going to take.**
   Try to find out from the teacher the answers to the following questions. Exactly what will the test cover? (grammar? speaking, listening, reading, writing? vocabulary? other?) Which topics will be the most important? What kind of items will be on the test? (multiple-choice? fill-in-the-blank? essay?) How long will it be?

2. **Create a plan of action for review.**
   If this is not the first test you have taken in this class, you should look at previous tests to find out what kind of test the teacher likes to give.

Organize your time before the test. Plan to spend enough time on review. Make sure those hours are not at one time and that you start reviewing several days before a test.

3. **Review the material.**

   Always skim through the textbook and any other materials the teacher has given you and look at your own written material and class notes. You can outline the major points and topics that are going to be covered on the test. You should also write down examples of the major points (for a grammatical point such as present perfect tense, you might write both the rule for it and several examples—the writing practice will help to practice a point). For a quick reminder just before the test, write the main points and topics on an index card.

4. **Take practice tests or do exercises.**

   Near the end of your reviewing time, it is important for you to do some self-practice. If your textbook has exercises in it that are similar to items that will be on the test, do some on your own as practice.

5. **Form a study group.**

   Many students benefit from studying for tests with other people. You might want to go through the reviewing process in strategy 3 with the help of other people. For part of your review with your group, quiz each other.

6. **Once you're ready, relax!**

   Good preparation is almost always the key to confidence. Confidence will lower your anxiety. High anxiety can prevent clear thinking during the test, so you want to make sure your anxiety is low. When you have done everything you can to prepare, relax and tell yourself, "I have now done my best to prepare. I believe in myself. I will perform well!"

   A good way to relax is to make sure you get a good night's sleep before a test. Make sure you keep your normal eating schedule before a test. You should also avoid medications that might slow down your thinking.

During the Classroom Test

It's test day. What should you do?

STRATEGIES FOR SUCCESS

1. **Get to the classroom early.**
   Arrive early enough to sit quietly in your seat, make yourself comfortable, and relax for a few minutes.

2. Look over the whole test.

When you get the test, quickly look over all the parts. Many people just start writing answers, but an overview is well worth one minute of your time.

3. Estimate your time.

Before you start answering questions, try to estimate how much time you will need for each part. If you budget your time, you will not run out of time, only to discover that you don't have time to respond to what may be the most important part of the test. You will need to check your watch or a clock several times during the test.

4. Focus.

As you take the test, try to focus on the tasks you must perform. Don't let noises or other people bother you. Don't let your mind wander.

5. Work carefully.

Work slowly enough so that you don't make careless errors. It's easy to make little mistakes, and you want your best performance to show on the test. As you write, try to notice what you are writing. Then, at the end, save some time to proofread your work so that you can correct little mistakes.

After the Classroom Test

It's easy to think that once a test is over, you can just forget it. However, the best students make sure that tests are *learning experiences*. They use a test and the feedback they get to help them to continue to improve their English. How can you turn your tests into learning experiences? Here are some ideas.

STRATEGIES FOR SUCCESS

1. Check yourself.

As soon as the test is over, go back to your notes and textbook and check yourself on anything you think you might not have done correctly. Review these topics right away. This will help to motivate you for the next test.

2. Pay attention in class to whatever the teacher says about the test answers.

When your teacher returns a test to you with feedback on what you did well and what you did not do well, make sure you pay attention in class to whatever the teacher says about the test answers. Take careful notes on the teacher's feedback.

3. Ask your teacher about specific points.

If your teacher does not give you enough feedback on your performance, you might ask about specific points on which you would like more information.

4. Make a plan to pay special attention.

Look at your notes and your test results and make a plan to pay special attention in the future to points that you are weak on. Make a list of the points, and in the next few days or weeks of study, give some special attention to those aspects of English.

Standardized Tests

You are probably familiar with standardized tests like the Test of English as a Foreign Language (TOEFL), the Test of English for International Communication (TOEIC), and college entrance examinations in English. They are different from classroom tests, so preparing for them sometimes requires different kinds of strategies. The strategies for classroom tests will help you, but some additional strategies are important, too.

First of all, remember that standardized tests measure *overall proficiency* (ability), so they are not based on a textbook or a course. On any one test, you can expect to see many different English grammar points, vocabulary, sounds, patterns, sentences, paragraphs, and conversations. So you cannot really study for these tests in the same way you study for classroom tests. Your best preparation is to be ready for the *types of items* on the test, the *skills* (usually listening and reading) involved, and the *time* factor.

If possible, find a book that tells you how to prepare for the standardized test. Many different books on the TOEFL and TOEIC tell you about what to expect on those tests. For other standardized tests, you may be able to get a simple guide that will tell you about the test. If you can get such a guide, make sure you go through all of it, including taking a practice test or two.

Here are some strategies for preparing for standardized tests.

STRATEGIES FOR SUCCESS

1. Be familiar with all the parts of the test.

2. Be familiar with all the types of items.

3. Read directions to the test and parts of the test very carefully.

4. When you are not sure of an answer on multiple-choice items (a, b, c, d, e), first cross out wrong answers and then guess the correct answer.

5. Do easier items first, because usually an easy item counts as much as a hard item.

6. If the test is designed so that leaving an answer blank counts as a wrong answer, then when time is running out, quickly guess the answers to items you haven't finished.

7. Watch your time carefully, and save time at the end to look over your answers.

5 Chapter 12

There are other differences in strategies for classroom tests and standardized tests. Your review time *before the test* is different because you cannot know exactly what English language points will be on the test, but learning what you can about the test and lowering anxiety through practice and preparation are still important. *During the test*, all five of the strategies listed here should still be followed. Unfortunately, *after the test*, you usually don't get feedback on your performance—all you get is a score, and it arrives as much as six weeks after you took the test!

The next time you take either a classroom test or a standardized test, following the suggestions in this chapter should improve your performance!

EXERCISES

Understanding Reading and Vocabulary

In this chapter, some important words are used that you must understand in order to use the information in the chapter. With a partner, guess the meaning of the underlined words from their context.

1. Before answering, I should <u>estimate</u> how much time the test will take.
2. During a test, I <u>concentrate</u> very carefully.
3. I pay attention to my teacher's <u>feedback</u> on the test.
4. Exactly what will the test <u>cover</u>?
5. An <u>overview</u> is well worth one minute of your time.
6. Don't make <u>careless</u> errors.
7. Standardized tests are designed to measure overall <u>proficiency</u>.
8. For <u>multiple-choice</u> items, guess the correct answer.

Speaking and Listening with a Partner

A. If there is a classroom test scheduled soon, then, with a partner, take the following steps:

1. Get all the information about the test that you can find.
2. Create a plan for reviewing the material.
3. Carry out the review carefully, sharing ideas and notes.
4. Take practice tests or exercises, then grade each other.

Soon after the test, get together again with your partner and talk about how you performed. Look up things that either of you think you didn't do well on. Review the items together. Make a short list of things you think you need to work on.

B. If there is not a classroom test scheduled soon, then, with a partner, take the following steps:

1. Look at Questionnaire 12 on pages 67–68. Choose three or four items on which you had a high (4 or 5) score.
2. Tell your partner what you have done, specifically, for each of the items in past tests. Take notes on what your partner tells you, especially if you had a low score on those items.
3. Find one or two items on which you had a low (1 or 2) score. Brainstorm with your partner some specific strategies for improving in those categories. Write your ideas down.
4. Use these ideas the next time you prepare for a test.

Discussing with the Whole Class

Tell the rest of the class about a strategy you use for helping you to do better on standardized tests, such as the TOEFL, the TOEIC, or a college entrance examination in English. Take notes on what each of your classmates says. Then make a Post-it of the strategies you think are the best to use.

Writing Your Journal

For the last entry in your journal, evaluate your success in following *Strategies for Success: A Practical Guide to Learning English*. Think about these questions:

1. How well did you follow the suggestions throughout the book?
2. Which chapters did you like best? Why?
3. Which chapters did you like least? Why?
4. What did you like—and/or not like—about working with a partner?
5. What did you like—and/or not like—about writing a journal?
6. Would you use this book again for another English class? Why or why not?

NOTES

NOTES

NOTES

NOTES

NOTES

80 ■

NOTES